UNDER THE
SACRED
CANOPY

About the Author

JD Walker (Greensboro, NC) is the vice chancellor of the House of Akasha, a North Carolina Pagan group. A former business journalist, she has written a regular garden column for various newspaper publications for over thirty years, including most recently *The Courier-Tribune* and *The Randolph Hub*. She also has contributed dozens of articles to Llewellyn's almanacs.

JD Walker

UNDER THE
SACRED
CANOPY

Working Magick
with the Mystical Trees
of the World

Llewellyn Publications
Woodbury, Minnesota

FIRST EDITION
First Printing, 2023

Book design by Christine Ha
Cover design by Shannon McKuhen
Interior art by the Llewellyn Art Department

Llewellyn Publications is a registered trademark of Llewellyn Worldwide Ltd.

Library of Congress Cataloging-in-Publication Data (Pending)
ISBN: 978-0-7387-6544-0

Llewellyn Publications
A Division of Llewellyn Worldwide Ltd.
2143 Wooddale Drive
Woodbury, MN 55125-2989
www.llewellyn.com

Printed in the United States of America

Also by JD Walker

A Witch's Guide to Wildcraft:
Using Common Plants to Create Uncommon Magick

Disclaimer

This book is not intended to provide medical advice or to take the place of medical advice and treatment from your personal physician. Readers are advised to consult their doctors or other qualified health-care professionals regarding the treatment of their medical problems. Neither the publisher nor the author takes any responsibility for any possible consequences from any treatment, action, or application of medicine, supplement, herb, or preparation to any person reading or following the information in this book.

Contents

Yggdrasil

Introduction

None of my friends were surprised when I told them I was writing a book about trees in an effort to better understand the concept of the Universe Tree. A surprising number of them didn't really know what a Universe Tree was—at least, the number surprised me. While ubiquitous, the Universe Tree can be a concept that isn't always obvious at first glance. In essence, in those cultures that had a Universe Tree as part of their mythology, it was thought to be a way of explaining how the entire world—from the abode of deities to the physical, everyday world to the land of the dead and otherworldly entities—worked. Explaining and sharing these mythologies and belief systems is the goal of this book.

My Quest

For many years, most people knew me as a lover of nature. I gardened. I taught classes on landscaping for homeowners. I wrote articles and advice columns on how to garden for almost three decades. During my career life as a reporter, I often wrote stories on the environment—specifically how a government or business action might impact the local environment. Many of my close friends knew me as a practicing Pagan. They were aware that I have contributed to *Llewellyn's Magical Almanac* and *Herbal Almanac* for years and that my first book, *A Witch's Guide to Wildcraft*, was published by the company in 2021. Knowing this, they wished me well in my efforts.

With that, the search was on to find out more about magickal trees in general and the Universe Tree in specific. I started this manuscript the same way I start anything I'm interested in—seeking to find more than I know in the moment about a particular topic or idea. While I know quite a bit about trees in the landscape, I didn't know as much as I wanted to know about the concept of the Universe Tree, something most people are familiar with as the World Tree. This sent me looking.

The information I found on legendary trees was staggering, at times overwhelming. I love mythology, so I have been aware of the many stories concerning sacred or magickal trees since before I could read. It all started with Mama reading us bedtime stories from a large book of such legends and fantasies. It moved on to visits to the local libraries, where I could check out collections of Greek and Roman mythology and Sumerian legends and European fairy tales and on and on.

In this particular search, I discovered a boatload of books on the topic. Some were general collections; others were in-depth studies of particular ethnic sagas. A few didn't deal specifically with a Cosmic Tree (another term for the Universe Tree concept that I was most interested in) but happened to include a little information about one legend or another.

Since a lot of my focus was on information regarding the Universe Tree, I was interested to discover quite a few articles and books that didn't discriminate between the idea of a Universe Tree and a Tree of Knowledge or a Tree of Life. These are very different concepts. Just because a certain tree provided a fruit or elixir for immortality, that doesn't make it a Universe Tree, for example.

That left an entire forest of trees with other special abilities, from Whomping Willows to trees of adventurous epics to magickal clothing wardrobes made of special apple trees that allow visitors to travel through other dimensions.

I also found a maddening number of stories that varied in one or more details when covering the same topic. For example, Trees of Life in the ancient Near East might have been a palm tree or a cypress or a rhubarb—any one of which could have been planted by any number of primary deities. Many reasons exist for the confusion. Part of it could be credited to translation. Different scholars might have different interpretations of a particular symbol or word or phrase.

Another factor is that societies borrowed from one another over time. One tradition's creation myth got picked up and mashed in with another's by a conquering horde or creative traveling minstrel. Or maybe the minstrel liked a bit of this story and a bit of that one. One evening over the campfire, they took some creative liberties. Who was going to stop a good storyteller, especially when it was early in humankind's history and the alternative to listening to the evening's story by the fire was going out in the darkness alone to get eaten by the first critter you encountered?

If it was a good story, it got repeated until, thousands of years later, an academic wrote it down. Or, at least, they wrote down the version they came across. Meanwhile, this person's peers were recording a slightly different version interpreted from the broken clay tablets they dug up. In any case, there are very few definitive versions of Universe Tree myths—or any myths, for that matter.

As mind-boggling as the number of recorded legends out there can be, equally frustrating was the lack of information on some traditional myths. This was especially true of the Slavic and Celtic myths. Frequently, I would read through sources in which a brief mention would be made of some society's concept of a tree that united heaven, earth, and the afterlife. That would be the end of it.

At first I thought the problem was carelessness on the part of the academic. As it turned out, the scholars frequently didn't include more information because the information isn't available—at least not in a fully constructed legend. All we have are bits and pieces of references in an ancient lullaby or a faint scratching on a funeral pot shard that kind of looks like a tree and could possibly be a sigil placed there to give the deceased a leg up on their way to the afterlife. Or not. It's not like the dead guy (or gal) is talking.

Shades of Gray

The result was that my effort to find more information on how some of our ancestors may have revered the trees in their life was very fruitful. My effort to find black-and-white answers to the question "What is the myth of the Universe Tree?" wasn't. I found answers, yes, but not so many "carved in stone." The answers could more easily be described as lovely shades of gray.

Here is what I have found: a goodly amount of information about the magickal influence of trees on societies through time, plus a better understanding of this concept I call the Universe Tree. As I will show in the upcoming pages, trees can and have been viewed as resources (both magickal and practical), spiritual entities in and of themselves, and concepts or ways to view the entire cosmos and all life therein.

As I looked at this wealth of information, I tried to sort it out in a general way by including discussions on how trees influenced our ancestors and why they may have related to trees in the manner that they did. I looked at how early people use trees and how can modern Pagans make use of them today. I have broken out many of the myths as they relate to trees—specifically some of the more common groups of trees that most people are likely to encounter in a modern environment.

I have gathered together basic information on many of the sacred trees from multiple sources from around the globe. While my aim was not to create an encyclopedia of magickal trees, I did want to share this forest of information that can be a jumping-off point for future research into more specific ethnic and cultural traditions.

I looked at the broader ideas concerning trees of life, trees of knowledge and wisdom, and, of course, the Universe Tree. This is what the reader will find in the coming chapters—stories from history and explanations from archeological records about what these trees are and how people of the past viewed them.

Finally, in the appendix, I've included some practical information on the trees we see around us—or might like to see around us if we have the time and space to cultivate our own spiritual arboretum.

Beneath the Universe Tree

I've tried to carry the idea of the Universe Tree forward into the present because I find the manner in which people today treat the myth is intriguing. No doubt the reader has seen countless representations of a Universe Tree on T-shirts, tapestries, book bags, and more. The Celtic tree in knotwork is especially prevalent. Ask any of those folks carrying or wearing it what that symbol means and the majority of them will say they think it comes from the environmental movement. There are also plenty of people who just think the design is pretty or clever and a few that understand the deeper meaning.

I found myself asking again and again, "Why are we so attached, so enamored with this symbol that we hang on our walls, display on our belongings, and wear on our bodies—often quite literally, as when we tattoo it permanently on our flesh?"

This seems like a missed opportunity in some way to me. Or maybe it is just personal hubris. Maybe I'm trying to force a deeper understanding where none is necessary. In all the reading I have done for this book, I came across a doctoral dissertation on the environmental impact of biological mass extinctions in modern times. The student took an in-depth look at what she called the "sixth great mass extinction" currently underway and her perceived sense that the current education system is failing to address the crisis.

Somehow in the midst of her study, she also found time to create a moving poem that begins with the line, "I confess to loving strong trees." She adds that she feels a sense of urgency to reclaim strong trees, to "learn their radical patience, their standing still, their lingering, here."[1]

The sentiments she expressed might adequately explain my urge to help promote a sense of the importance we can attribute to the Universe Tree symbol in our lives, in our world today, and to trees in general.

The modern world could use a reminder of the magickal impact trees have in our lives, in my opinion. If remembering the myths about dryads who live in oak trees makes us think twice about harming a stately oak on our property, that's a good thing—again, in my opinion.

But when it comes to the origin of the world, we don't need a Universe Tree to explain how the world was created. We have stellar

---

1. Susan Reed, "In/appropriate Education in a Time of Mass Extinction: Composing a Methodological Imbroglio of Love and Grief," EdD diss., Appalachian State University, 2015, 185.

telescopes and geological surveys and archaeological digs to provide those answers.

We do, however, need something that helps us better understand our place in the world. We need something that helps us accept our place in the world and our connection to all the other components of that world, both sentient and non-sentient. A larger-than-life, non-preachy, non-condemning, universally accepting and accepted concept that anyone can understand. A thing that doesn't oppress anyone, the understanding of which can benefit everyone.

Something that when pointed to with a facial expression of openness and a welcoming wave of the hand regardless of language barriers says, "Meet me, sister. Meet me, brother, beneath the Universe Tree and let us simply be."

This can't be too much to ask.

Ankerwycke

Chapter 1
Humans and Trees—
A Unique Relationship

The story of trees is bound up in a general tendency of world populations to see and recognize trees as crucial to survival, making them sacred and magickal. To say that all human cultures have venerated trees at some point would not be far off the mark. Carl Jung, in associating the collective unconscious with a tree, opined that humans could not help but venerate trees.

In his *Zarathustra* seminar, Jung stated that the very human consciousness comes from the tree and then dissolves back into the tree again. In that consciousness, the tree provides the nourishment for the stars and is the origin of the primordial parents of humanity. Humans might have seized on an animal or the earth itself as a metaphor, Jung said, "but no, it is the tree, and the tree means something specific; that is a peculiar symbol."[2]

Veneration of Trees through Time

To that end, myths and stories exist about trees of wisdom, trees of wealth, and trees of immortality. Then there are scores of stories

---

2. Carl Jung, *Nietzsche's "Zarathustra": Notes of the Seminar Given in 1934–1939*, vol. 2, ed. James L. Jarrett (Princeton, NJ: Princeton University Press, 1988), 1432.

about this woman or that man being turned into a special type of tree either as punishment or as protection from the unwanted advances of some deity. These are the trees of legend that stand under the canopy of the Universe Tree but are not actually Universe Trees.

Additionally, we have trees of history. Many European cultures once identified with specific trees. Historian J. A. MacCulloch wrote that certain Celtic tribes were identified by the trees they held sacred, such as the *Eburones* (the yew tree tribe), while some surnames indicated that a family held sacred a particular tree. Writing at the beginning of the twentieth century in Scotland, MacCulloch was the preeminent historian of his day on Celtic history. He pointed out the etymology of surnames like *Vivisci* (men of the mistletoe) and *Guerngen* (son of the alder).[3] These trees were thought to carry the history of the tribe, given the trees' longevity. They provided access to medicine and magick. They might have been a conduit to a tribal deity. They would certainly have been held in esteem because of the food and shelter they provided. Tribal trees might be argued to have been the center of the world for the people who revered them—in Greek language they would be the *omphalos*, or navel of the earth.

Large, old trees have taken on significance in many cultures. The venerable yew at Runnymede in England, called the Ankerwycke Yew, is believed to have been old when King John signed the Magna Carta in a meeting under its branches.[4] Even before that historic event, people in the region believed it was the site where druids would gather for their rituals.

---

3. J. A. MacCulloch, *The Religion of the Ancient Celts* (Mineola, NY: Dover Publications, 2003), 202.
4. Marissa Fessenden, "Legend Says the Ankerwycke Yew Witnessed the Magna Carta's Signing," *Smithsonian Magazine*, February 20, 2015, https://www .smithsonianmag.com/smart-news/legend-says-ankerwycke-yew-witnessed -signing-magna-carta-180954373/.

In Lebanon, 16 trees make up an olive grove that is believed to be over 5,000 years old. The trees are still in production for olives and olive oil. According to the folklore of the area, the dove that flew from Noah's boat plucked an olive branch from one of these trees, signifying the promise that the Great Flood was over.[5]

Near Tokyo, Japan, at the Shinto Sugawara Shrine, the Great Sugi of Kayano is a *Cryptomeria* tree that is believed to be over 2,000 years old and is protected by the Japanese government as a natural monument. The tree is thought to have been planted by humans at the shrine, which honors the Shinto god of scholarship, Tenjin.

The effort to recognize and preserve old trees is carried on today. In the United States, we call them "witness trees." These are trees that grow on the sites of important battles and historical gatherings in our nation's history. Special efforts are made to ensure the trees are protected from encroachment and damage. Examples of these trees include the Jackson magnolia (*Magnolia grandiflora*) planted at the south portico of the White House by the seventh president, Andrew Jackson, in memory of his wife, Rachel, who died before his inauguration in 1829. It can be seen on the back of US $20 bills printed between 1929 and 1999.[6]

Another witness tree with a somber history stands on the site of the First and Second Battles of Manassas in Virginia during the American Civil War in what is now the Manassas National Battleground Park. It is a towering white oak (*Quercus alba*). The tree

5. Tara Vassiliou, "Epic Olive Trees," Olive Oil Times, June 10, 2012, https://www.oliveoiltimes.com/world/epic-olive-trees/26998.
6. Mike Townsend, "Silent Sentinels of Storied Landscapes," National Park Service, National Mall and Memorial Parks, July 24, 2012, https://www.nps.gov/nama/blogs/silent-sentinels-of-storied-landscapes.htm; "Denominations: $20," US Currency Education Program, accessed May 20, 2022, https://www.uscurrency.gov/denominations/20.

oversaw the carnage as soldiers from the North and South fought and died.[7]

Internationally, these are called heritage trees, and they receive special designation by organizations like UNESCO World Heritage Centre.

This illustrates the regard for trees that endures even today. Being able to touch an organism that has lived for hundreds if not thousands of years is evocative, regardless of your personal beliefs.

Beyond Real-World Trees

Magickal trees number in the hundreds. Universe Trees are few in number and often associated with other terms, specifically world pillar, *axis mundi*, and *imago mundi*. Carole Cusack is a religious scholar at the University of Sydney, Australia, who specializes in early medieval Europe, Western esotericism, and contemporary religion. According to Cusack, "Ancient Pagans believed trees could express profound cosmological and spiritual truths; they were frequently connected to the image of the world (*imago mundi*), which often took the form of a giant human being, and to the notion of the centre (*axis mundi*), which both mapped territory and connected the earth to the heavens above and the underworld below."[8]

In other words, as the center of a particular ancient society's universe or world, a sacred tree could also be viewed as a pillar around which the entire world revolved. In fact, some scholars have suggested that the great central wooden pillars that were erected in the

---

7. Mike Yessis, "These Five 'Witness Trees' Were Present at Key Moments in America's History," *Smithsonian Magazine*, August 25, 2017, https://www.smithsonianmag.com/travel/these-five-witness-trees-were-present-at-key-moments-in-americas-history-180963925/.

8. Carole M. Cusack, *The Sacred Tree: Ancient and Medieval Manifestations* (Newcastle upon Tyne, UK: Cambridge Scholars Publishing, 2011), xiv–xv.

gathering spaces of Germanic tribes may have started out as actual trees—usually giant oaks—before the people eventually moved to a more practical approach of using one huge trunk to represent the center of their world.

This is the literal "axis mundi," or world pole, and is represented perfectly by Irminsul, the tribal pole erected to honor the Saxon god Irmin. Different sources indicate Irmin may have been subsumed by worship of Tyr, who was in time replaced in importance by Wodin, who is often conflated with Odin.

Regardless, *Irminsul* apparently didn't refer to one specific pole in one specific place.[9] It was to be found everywhere. According to sources, an Irminsul, or "great pole," could and probably was set up wherever Saxon tribes would congregate in sacred groves and forests.[10] It was generally wood but could also be a stone pillar.

Quite a few Christian saints and rulers made a name for themselves by chopping down or digging up the Irminsul of a tribe they wished to subdue. The most famous example is that of Charlemagne, who destroyed an Irminsul in the Teutoburg Forest in Saxony in Northwest Germany in or about 772 CE in order to cow the Saxons.[11] To be transparent, some historical sources indicate Charlemagne was responding to the burning of an area church by a Saxon tribe.

In all likelihood, the decision was pretext for subjugating the pagan tribes of the region. Charlemagne wasn't known for a modest appetite when it came to expanding his empire.

9. Ruth Mazo Karras, "Pagan Survivals and Syncretism in the Conversion of Saxony," *The Catholic Historical Review* 72, no. 4 (1986): 563, http://www.jstor.org/stable/25022405.

10. Sidney E. Dean, "Felling the Irminsul: Charlemagne's Saxon Wars." *Medieval Warfare* 5, no. 2 (2015): 16, https://www.jstor.org/stable/48578430.

11. Sidney E. Dean, "Felling the Irminsul: Charlemagne's Saxon Wars." *Medieval Warfare* 5, no. 2 (2015): 16, https://www.jstor.org/stable/48578430.

The Spirit of Trees Sprouts Again

As we examine the history of modern Western Pagan traditions of the past 60 or so years, the leaders of the new Pagan renaissance were probably aware of the importance trees had to some people in the past as they began to rediscover the history and traditions of ancient religions. However, as chance would have it, the returning interest in early pagan traditions caught hold and took off at the same time as popular support for environmental protection. When more conservative groups complained about "hippies" and "tree huggers," they really didn't draw a hard distinction between those folks and the people who were trying to reconstruct old pagan traditions. I know. I lived it, as did many in my generation coming of age in the 1960s and '70s.

My mother and grandmother knew of my interest in the occult as I went off to college. Every time I headed out the door and back to the dorm, Grandma would earnestly warn me to "watch out for those hippies." In her mind, Pagans and hippies (or other radicals) were one and the same.

As such, the modern meaning of the Universe Tree and sacred trees in general has become a bit muddled. Trees are sacred, yes. Trees are important, certainly. But press the average person (Pagan or otherwise) hard enough, and they probably won't be able to tell you why this is true or how it came to be true.

Most people will understand that trees are nice to have around. They have something to do with providing oxygen for us, lumber for our homes, and paper for our books. But, beyond that, people aren't really sure why trees should matter.

For people who begin to contemplate the Universe Tree, it's almost like waking up in a fog with a mild case of amnesia. I am reminded of a story that is told about Ronald Reagan when he left the White House and eventually succumbed to the ravages of Alzheimer's disease. Toward the end of his life, like many of those consumed by Alzheimer's, Reagan lived but didn't relate to everyday happenings. At one point, his wife, Nancy, found Reagan standing in a room in their home holding a small ceramic replica of the White House. He had pulled it out of the fish tank. When she asked him what it was, he reportedly said, "I don't know, but I think it's something to do with me."[12]

Regardless of your political persuasion, this is a sad story and a little frightening. Still, it illustrates the point when contemplating the impact of trees in our lives. We understand this thing—this large, colorful, silent, arboreal thing—has something important to do with us.

Most of us just aren't certain what that is.

---

12. Rebecca Leung, "Morris: 'Reagan Still a Mystery,'" 60 Minutes, CBS News, June 9, 2004, https://www.cbsnews.com/news/morris-reagan-still-a-mystery/.

Jubokko

Chapter 2
Trees, Tree Spirits, and More

Before looking at the larger concepts of the Universe Tree, let's take a moment to look at how people have seen the magickal aspect of trees in their immediate landscapes. Humans can tend to fall into the habit of seeing everything in the universe as revolving around them and their needs. We have frequently been taught that plants were put here for our benefit.

This isn't exactly true. Plants can benefit us, particularly trees. However, all plants have a unique energy, and they're not just here to be a resource for humans. Trees have an inherent energy that you can learn to feel if you devote a little time to meditating with these arboreal giants.

In the past, people believed that certain trees were spiritual entities, in and of themselves. In some cases, these spirits could be enticed to be protectors of humans. In other cases, the spirits definitely did not want to have anything to do with humans or were openly hostile to them.

Tree Spirits around the World

What follows are examples of magickal trees, tree spirits, and deities from around the world. Some are ancient. Some are modern creations but ones that have become ubiquitous in the grove of the Universe Tree. This is not an exhaustive list. It is more to whet the appetite and demonstrate yet again that humans have a love affair with trees that stretches over time and across many lands.

Apple Tree Man (England)

In certain areas of England, the oldest apple tree in the orchard is said to be inhabited by a spirit called the apple tree man. He oversees the production of the orchard. Those respectful orchard owners who honor the apple tree man may be allowed to share in his golden treasure, secreted somewhere in the orchard.

Baucis and Philemon (Greece/Rome)

Baucis and Philemon were an old couple of meager means who lived near the region of Tyana. One day, Jupiter and Mercury disguised themselves as travelers and went through a village in the region. Everywhere they were refused hospitality until they arrived at the hovel of Baucis and Philemon. The old couple welcomed the travelers warmly and graciously prepared what they could from their paltry resources. After some conversation, they realized their traveling guests were divine and pleaded for forgiveness for their rough offerings. Jupiter reassured them and told the old couple to follow him up to the top of a nearby hill. From the top, the couple could see that the entire village, except for their home, had been flooded. Jupiter turned their home into a grand temple where Baucis and Philemon served as priests until the day they died. At the very moment of their death, both were turned into trees.[13] Basing his work on that of the Roman poet Ovid, American author Thomas Bulfinch didn't say what type of tree the two turned into. Writing roughly 60 years later, American author and educator Edith Hamilton recorded that

---

13. Thomas Bulfinch, *The Age of Fable* (New York: New American Library, 1962), 80.

the pair turned into a linden (*Tilia*) and an oak (*Quercus*) that grew from a single trunk.[14]

Bitâbohs (Sudan)

Bitâbohs are dark, evil spirits that haunt gloomy forests in the Southern Sudan region of Africa.[15]

Cyparissus (Greece)

Cyparissus was a favorite of Apollo. Some say he was one of the god's many lovers. Apollo gifted Cyparissus a tame stag. One day, by accident, Cyparissus killed his beloved stag. He was so overcome by grief, he prayed to the gods, saying he wished to forever mourn his loss. The gods obliged by turning him into a cypress tree, which is why the cypress is often associated with death and loss.[16]

Crann Bethadh (Ireland)

This is most often seen as an oak. The *Crann Bethadh* unites all the worlds from heaven to earth to the underworld, making this yet another example of a Universe Tree. While sources indicate the Celts of Ireland always saw trees as magickal and wonderous in general, some scholars suggest the concept of a Universe Tree similar to

14. Edith Hamilton, *Mythology: Timeless Tales of Gods and Heroes* (New York: New American Library, 1940; repr. New York: Little, Brown & Company, 1969), 113.

15. Folkard, Robert, *Plant Lore, Legends, and Lyrics* (London: R. Folkard & Sons, 1884), 88.

16. Ovid, *Metamorphoses*, trans. A. S. Kline (electronic reproduction, University of Virginia, 2000), book 10, 106–42, https://ovid.lib.virginia.edu/trans /Metamorph10.htm#484521420.

Yggdrasil might have come with Northern invaders during the many migrations of those people into the British Isles.[17]

Dripping Ancient Hazel (Ireland)

While hazelnut trees were generally held in high esteem, one developed a particularly bad reputation.[18] When Lugh battled Balor of the Evil Eye in the second Battle of Mag Tuired (*Magh Tuireadh*), he bested the Fomorian and cut off his head. According to some interpretations of the legend, Lugh hung the head in a nearby hazel tree. As the head dripped, it poisoned the tree and the location, making it a gloomy place where only vultures and ravens hung out. When the tree was eventually dug out, nine men died from the poisonous fumes in the process of excavating the plant. Finn McCool's magickal shield was said to have been carved from the wood of the tree.

Dryope (Thebes)

Dryope was a human who mistakenly picked the flowers of a lotus tree. She didn't know that the tree was inhabited by the nymph Lotis. The tree began to bleed and the blood touched Dryope's skin. From that point, she was doomed. She quickly began to change into a black poplar tree. She had just enough time to warn her husband

---

17. Ellen Lloyd, "Celtic Tree of Life—Portal to Invisible Worlds and Source of Sacred Knowledge," Ancient Pages, July 26, 2021, https://www.ancientpages .com/2021/07/26/celtic-tree-of-life-portal-to-invisible-worlds-and-source-of -sacred-knowledge/.

18. Eleanor Hull, ed., *The Poem Book of the Gael, Translations from Irish Gaelic Poetry into English Prose and Verse* (London: Chatto & Windus, 1913; Project Gutenberg, 2014), xxvii, https://www.gutenberg.org/files/46917/46917 -h/46917-h.htm.

not to pick the flowers and to beg him to take care of their son before she was completely transformed.[19]

Dryads (Greece)

Dryads are spiritual entities who protect trees. They are usually seen in human form. The word *dryad* literally translates to "oak," but over time, it has become associated with tree spirits in general. There were many known by name, including Daphne, who is associated with laurels; Dryope, associated with oaks; and Erato, a priestess of Pan, god of the wooded glen. Some groups of dryads tended to congregate around specific species.

Ent (Britain)

Ents are shepherds of certain forests in J. R. R. Tolkien's series of books on Middle Earth. They are ancient and over time have grown to look like the trees they protect, but they aren't spirits. They were created by the fairy queen Yavanna at the beginning of time to protect trees from overharvesting by dwarves. In the Lord of the Rings series, the Ent Treebeard compares Ents to Huorns.

Erysichthon (Greece)

Erysichthon was a wretched human who dared to cut down a dryad-occupied tree in a grove sacred to Ceres.[20] For his crime, he was cursed with insatiable hunger. He sold everything he had to buy food. Finally, he had nothing left but his own daughter. He tried to sell her, but the girl appealed to Neptune, her former lover, for help. Neptune gave her the ability to change into any animal at will to help her

---

19. Ovid, *Metamorphoses*, trans. Rolfe Humphries (Bloomington: Indiana University Press, 1955), 235.
20. Ovid, *Metamorphoses*, trans. Rolfe Humphries (Bloomington: Indiana University Press, 1955), 204.

evade servitude. Sadly, the girl went back to her father every time, who continued to sell her over and over again. Finally in desperation, he began to eat his own flesh until there was nothing left of him.

Fabled Pine of Tokyo (Japan)

The Fabled Pine (*Pinus thunbergii*) stands in the Matsudaira Garden in Tokyo and is believed to be almost 600 years old. It has survived storms, fires, and earthquakes. Visitors to the park pay homage to the tree and bow to it as they pass by.[21]

Fighting Trees of Oz

The fighting trees in Frank Baum's Oz series are grumpy beings who live at the edge of the enchanted forest to the south of the City of Oz. Their job is to guard the forest and keep the uninvited out. They can't walk but they can flex their branches to grab passersby.

Grandmother Cedar (Cedar Grandmother)

The Ojibwe associate the white cedar (*Thuja occidentalis*) with the direction of south. According to their legend, the Creator came to Grandmother Cedar and asked her to work with his "two-leggeds," the people he had made. He asked her to teach them how to use the cedar for medicine when they became ill. She also showed the Creator's people how to use the tree's inner bark for shelter, baskets, clothing, and more.[22] Her service to the tribes was especially valued because she gave of herself, voluntarily.

---

21. Glenn Moore and Cassandra Atherton, "Eternal Forests: The Veneration of Old Trees in Japan," *Arnoldia* 77, no. 4 (2020): 26–27, https://arboretum .harvard.edu/wp-content/uploads/2020/06/2020-77-4-Arnoldia.pdf.

22. Lillian Pitawanakwat, "Ojibwe/Powawatomi (Anishinabe) Teaching," FourDirectionsTeachings.com, accessed June 15, 2022, http://www .fourdirectionsteachings.com/transcripts/ojibwe.html.

Grandmother Willow

When Pocahontas needs advice in Disney's animated film of the same name, she turns to the ancient Grandmother Willow. This is a storyteller's fantasy and not based on a particular Native American legend. In the animated feature, Grandmother Willow represents the spirit of nature. She is wise and yet playful, as she coaches Pocahontas through her first encounter with Captain John Smith and future interactions with the English colonists.

Hamadryads (Greece)

In some sources, hamadryads are equated with dryads. In others, they literally embody the tree with which they are associated. To harm the tree was to harm the spirit within. In legends, when some foolish mortal cuts down a spirit-inhabited tree, it moans and bleeds real blood before it dies.[23]

Huntin (West Africa)

The *huntin* is a tree deity that inhabits special silk cotton trees. When identified, local natives designate it with a girdle of palm tree leaves. Offerings to the tree include birds that are laid at its base. This particular tree must not be harmed. Any other silk cotton tree must be honored with sacrifices of poultry and palm oil before being cut down.[24]

---

23. Edith Hamilton, *Mythology: Timeless Tales of Gods and Heroes* (New York: New American Library, 1940; repr. New York: Little, Brown & Company, 1969), 42.
24. James Frazer, *The Golden Bough: A Study in Magic and Religion* (New York: Macmillan, 1922; electronic reproduction, Bartleby.com, 2000), 112, www.bartleby.com/196/.

Huorn (Britain)

Like the Ents, Huorns are a creation of J. R. R. Tolkien. They aren't trees but they aren't Ents, either. And, like the Ents, they have spent so much time in the forest that they look like trees. They definitely have an attitude problem when it comes to outsiders in their forest. Their anger is driven by the actions of Orcs who decimated the trees there. To avoid any future invasions, the Huorns tend to attack anyone who enters their sphere of influence first and ask questions later.

Jubokko (Japan)

The *jubokko* are Japanese vampire trees. In battlefields where there was major loss of life and blood saturated the ground, the trees there were said to develop a taste for blood. Over time, they would grab any poor victim who wandered too close, draining them of all their blood. There is some argument about whether this is a proper tree spirit or just a tree that is inhabited by a *yōkai*, a generic animating spirit that could take over just about anything. The concept of the jubokko was popularized by the modern Japanese manga artist Shigeru Mizuki and may have been developed by him.

Kalpa (India)

Also known as the *Kalpavriksha* or wishing tree, this was considered to be a food source for the first humans. In some Indian traditions, the Kalpa Tree is also considered to be a Universe Tree connecting the mundane world with both heaven and the underworld. It is said to be planted at the peak of Mount Meru in the middle of five gardens of paradise.[25]

---

25. A. Sutherland, "Kalpa Tree 'Kalpavriksha': The Sacred Wishing Tree Has Been Object of Adornment and Worship Since Ancient Times," Ancient Pages, July 22, 2016, https://www.ancientpages.com/2016/07/22/kalpa-tree -kalpavriksha-the-sacred-wishing-tree-has-been-object-of-adornment-and -worship-since-ancient-times/.

Kodama (Japan)

These are the tree spirits of Japan. They seem to inhabit particularly old trees, giving each tree its own personality. To cut down a tree occupied by a *kodama* was to invite the wrath of an angry spirit.[26]

Lorax (United States)

Author Theodor Seuss Geisel (a.k.a. Dr. Seuss) created the story of the Lorax in his 1971 book of the same name. The Lorax "speaks for the trees" in the book, trying to stop the destruction of a forest of Truffula Trees by a thoughtless industrialist. Sadly, the Lorax doesn't succeed in his arguments. The industrialist learns too late that his greed has resulted in the total devastation of the local environment. Geisel didn't specifically describe the Lorax as a tree spirit, but the creature does spring from the stump of the first Truffula Tree that is cut down. When the last tree of the forest falls, he gives the industrialist a sad backward glance as he rises into the sky by lifting himself by the seat of his pants. He leaves a warning of "Unless" written in stone. The industrialist eventually understands this as a moral: Unless someone cares, nothing will get better. Nothing at all.[27]

Maliades (Greece)

These are dryads associated with fruit orchards. The guardians of the golden apples in the Gardens of Hesperides were maliades. The three maidens were daughters of Hesperus and were named Hespera, Aegle, and Erytheis.[28] They were supposed to guard and tend the

---

26. Glenn Moore and Cassandra Atherton, "Eternal Forests: The Veneration of Old Trees in Japan," *Arnoldia* 77, no. 4 (2020): 25, https://arboretum.harvard.edu/wp-content/uploads/2020/06/2020-77-4-Arnoldia.pdf.

27. Theodore Seuss Geisel, *The Lorax* (New York: Random House, 1971).

28. Arthur Cotterell and Rachel Storm, *The Ultimate Encyclopedia of Mythology* (New York: Hermes House, 2002), 54.

apples but got caught eating them by Hera. Hera put a stop to that by installing a giant serpent (or possibly a dragon) around the tree.

Moss Woman (Germany)

The moss woman of Central Germany is covered and clothed in moss. She is a forest spirit who might be inclined to help the industrious farmer near her forest, even so much as to help him prosper.[29]

Myrrha (Greece)

Myrrha was the mother of Adonis, a boy who would grow up to be the most beautiful man in the world. But he was conceived by a wicked act.[30] Myrrha loved her father, Cinyras. She tricked him into sleeping with her him and became pregnant. When he realized what had happened, Cinyras chased her all the way to the Arabian Peninsula. Myrrha pleaded with the gods to save her. They took pity on her, changing her into a myrrh tree. She was still able to give birth to the boy, however, and the droplets of myrrh resin that ooze from the tree are said to be her tears.

Nariphon (Thailand)

This is a magickal tree that grows in the legendary forest of Himaphan in the Himalayas. It was created by the god Indra as a distraction for the hermits in the area, to protect Vessantara's wife, Madri, when she was alone. Despite training, the hermits had not entirely overcome their lustful desires. When Madri wanted to go into the forest, Indra made the Nariphon tree produce fruit that

---

29. J. H. Philpot, *The Sacred Tree: or, The Tree in Religion and Myth* (London: Macmillan, 1897; Project Gutenberg, 2014), 51, https://www.gutenberg.org /files/47215/47215-h/47215-h.htm.
30. Ovid, *Metamorphoses*, trans. Rolfe Humphries (Bloomington: Indiana University Press, 1955), 243.

looked just like a young maiden. The hermits would pick the fruit and carry it off to satisfy their amorous desires, leaving Madri safe in the forest.

Philyra (Greece)

By some accounts, Philyra was the mother of the centaur Chiron by Cronos. Cronos courted Philyra while in the guise of a stallion, which explains why the couple's son comes out as half-human and half-horse. Philyra had no love for her son and abandoned him. She pleaded with Zeus to turn her into anything other than human so that she wouldn't have to abide the horror of her son. Zeus obliged by turning her into a linden tree (*Tilia*).

Pontianak (Malaysia)

Pontianak is one of many names given to vampire spirits that can occupy the frangipani tree (*Plumeria*). Appearing as beautiful women dressed in white with long fingernails and red eyes, they are believed to drink the blood and eat the vital organs of men they latch on to.[31] They can only come out during a full moon.

Sykeus (Greece)

Sykeus (sometimes Syceus) was one of the Titans who fought against Zeus and the rest of the Greek pantheon for control of the world. Zeus chased him to Cilicia, where Sykeus begged his mother, Gaia, to hide him. She turned him into the world's first fig tree.[32] The Greek word for "fig" is *sykon*.

---

31. Reuters Staff, "FACTBOX—Haunted Bananas: Asia's Spirit-Infested Trees," Reuters, September 24, 2007, https://www.reuters.com/article/us-singapore -trees-factbox/factbox-haunted-bananas-asias-spirit-infested-trees -idUSSP16223720070924.

32. "Sykeus," Theoi Project, accessed October 1, 2021, https://www.theoi.com /Gigante/GiganteSykeus.html.

Tree of Peace (North America/Iroquois Nation)

The Tree of Peace was an actual tree used to symbolize the unity of the five tribes of the Iroquois Nation, including the Mohawk, Seneca, Cayuga, Onondaga, and Oneida tribes. These were eventually joined by the Tuscarora.[33] In the fifteenth century, the Indian leader Dekanawida planted a white pine (*Pinus strobus*) after the tribes came together to form their nation. It was set somewhere in New York near Lake Ontario. In some tellings of the legend, a tree was first uprooted so that warring factions could toss their weapons under it and fight no more.[34] This could be where we get the saying "to bury the hatchet."

Waldgeist (Germany)

The waldgeist is a spirit believed to guard and protect the forests of Germany. The waldgeist is usually seen as an old man, sometimes mischievous but generally kind if you are respectful of the forest it protects. In some cases, he might even grant a wish to the true of heart.[35]

Whomping Willow (Britain)

The Whomping Willow is the enchanted guardian tree in the Harry Potter series. It's a little unclear whether the willow is naturally enchanted or if it is an ordinary willow planted on the property and then enchanted by Professor Sprout. Regardless, it does a wicked job

---

33. "Tree of Peace," National Park Service, last modified April 27, 2022, https://www.nps.gov/articles/tree-of-peace.htm.

34. "Tree of Peace: The Iroquois Legend of the Eastern White Pine," accessed December 17, 2021, Northeastern Lumber Manufacturers Association, https://www.nelma.org/tree-of-peace-the-iroquois-legend-of-the-eastern-white-pine/.

35. "Waldgeist," Academic Dictionaries and Encyclopedias, accessed September 1, 2021, https://en-academic.com/dic.nsf/enwiki/3750159.

of keeping everyone away from an entrance to a tunnel that leads to a safe place where Remus Lupin can change into a werewolf.

Zapis (Serbia)

Zapis is the general name for a sacred tree in Serbia. Villagers would gather around the zapis for worship, trials, and weddings. It was frequently an oak but could be other tree species. A cross was often incised into the bark, and the local priest would lead ceremonies such as laying food and flower offerings around the tree in exchange for its protection of the village and its inhabitants.[36] Serbian historian and scholar Veselin Čajkanović (1881–1945) wrote that the practice was adopted by Christians from much older religious beliefs. Sometimes the villagers would also erect an altar at or near the base of the tree. It was forbidden to cut down or damage the village zapis.

Zaqquum (Saudi Arabia)

Zaqquum is a tree that grows in the fiery lake of hell. The flowers look like the faces of devils. The fruit on the tree is generated from the misdeeds and wickedness of the sinners who inhabit hell. Sinners are forced to eat the fruit, which boils in their stomachs like lye.[37]

Working with Tree Spirits

If we believe that trees have some type of sentience, can we reach out to them? If we believe a tree has an associated spirit, is it possible to establish a connection? The answer to both questions is yes.

---

36. "Belief in a Holy Tree—Zapis," Britić, December 24, 2015, https://www .britic.co.uk/2015/12/24/belief-in-a-holy-tree-zapis/.

37. Rashad Khalifa, trans., *Quran: The Final Testament* (Tucson, AZ: United Submitters International, 1990), 300.

I regularly ask the ancient spirits (arboreal, divine, and human) around my house to be with me and protect me and mine from harm. That could be the harm from unwanted visitors or the harm from a storm. From time to time, I might ask for their help in my ritual or spell work. It's all in how you ask.

To evoke the help of the trees around you, first establish a connection to the plant. Ask it if it will consider helping you. I've only had a few encounters with trees that seem to indicate to me they weren't interested. That's fine. I thanked the tree in question and never bothered it again.

Those that seem to be inclined to help, or at least listen, seem to appreciate what little help I can give them. This comes in the form of keeping the area around it tidy, clearing away debris, and, if necessary, pruning any damage that occurs to the plant. Leaving offerings around the tree is helpful. I have a friend who routinely empties the water from her ritual bowl around a tree in front of her business. In exchange, she asks for its protection and positive energy for her business. It seems to be a good working arrangement.

From time to time, it helps to simply sit with the tree. Talk to it. Tell it about your day, your hopes, your travails, your successes. This is good therapy for you and it might be entertaining for the tree.

If you want to reach out to specific spirits associated with the trees around you, first be careful who you reach out to. For example, why would you want to reach out to the Zaqquum? What possible benefit could this be for you? Second, keep in mind that just because you want to talk with the spirit, that doesn't mean the spirit wants to talk to you. You can ask. But don't be surprised if you don't get an answer or if the answer is no.

As with any entity beyond the mundane world, it helps to know what that entity likes. For example, if you want to reach out to the moss woman, I imagine she might like a variety of mosses as a gift.

If you wanted to reach out to the apple tree man, it seems he appreciates it when his orchard is well tended.

Most of all, show your respect for your environment. Trashing the area around your home isn't going to win you any points with the wildlife or the associated spirits there. And be patient. Many trees outlive us by decades. The spirits associated with them are eternal. Our modern world may be based on instant gratification; theirs is not. Take the time to know your environment and the spirits there. The eventual contact you achieve is the reward for your patience.

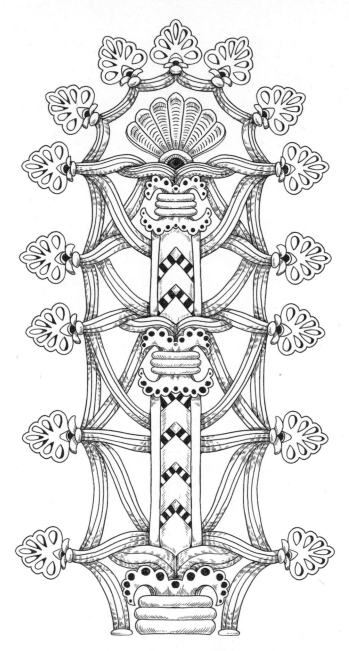

Sumerian Tree of Life

Chapter 3
Trees of Life

We've looked at trees in the mundane world and a sprinkling of trees imbued with a spirit, whether one that inhabits them or a specific life force that becomes a personality in its own right. Going forward, it's time to look in more detail at three specific types of trees: Trees of Life, Trees of Knowledge or Wisdom, and the overarching concept of the Universe Tree.

I'll begin with the Tree of Life. Think of the Tree of Life as an origin story or a source of sustainability for all life. Deities don't live there, although some pantheons do gather beneath it to discuss worldly business. Some supernatural entities may tend or guard it. Humankind certainly doesn't live under it. In fact, people are frequently forbidden access to it.

Based on the myths and legends we have that have been passed down through time, for the people who lived thousands of years ago these stories might be considered the equivalent to our big bang theory. The universe has to start somewhere.

For modern theorists, our universe began 13.8 billion years ago from a point of singularity of infinite density. For some reason, it exploded in a big bang. It has been racing out in all directions ever since and will do so indefinitely—maybe. Shortly before he died, English physicist Stephen Hawking took the stance that the ongoing expansion isn't infinite—that at some point the universe will collapse back on itself. In this model, the universe is a complex hologram.[38]

It's an intriguing theory, and I am certainly in no position to discuss the science behind it. One should point out also that physicists are already pushing the concept of origin back beyond the initial "bang."[39]

Early rationales for how life began just illustrate that humankind has always had a deep-seated need to explain how we got here. For certain cultures it all begins with a tree. In some cases, the tree is the origin of all life; in other cases, it is only the source of human life. In still other global myths, the tree is the sustainer of life. In the first instances, once life is seeded, whether all life or just human life, the tree has done its business and is simply an explanation of where we all come from. It no longer exists. In the second case, the tree still exists and through its continued existence, life as we know it continues. That carries with it the warning that, if the Tree of Life is destroyed, life as we know it will be destroyed as well. Yggdrasil is the classic example of this. However, there are many more options for explaining the beginning of life at the base of a tree.

What follows is a look at the way a number of different cultures around the world utilized the Tree of Life myth. Keep in mind— a lot of blending and borrowing of myths occurs especially in the area of the Middle East. This discussion isn't meant to declare whose

38. Matt Williams, "Here's Stephen Hawking's Final Theory about the Big Bang," Universe Today, May 4, 2018, https://www.universetoday.com/139167/heres -stephen-hawkings-final-theory-about-the-big-bang/; Stephen Hawking and Thomas Hertog, "A Smooth Exit from Eternal Inflation?," University of Leuven, Belgium, April 20, 2018, 4, https://arxiv.org/pdf/1707.07702.pdf.
39. Ethan Siegal, "These 4 Pieces of Evidence Have Already Taken Us Beyond the Big Bang," Forbes, February 21, 2020, https://www.forbes.com/sites /startswithabang/2020/02/21/these-4-pieces-of-evidence-have-already -taken-us-beyond-the-big-bang/?sh=32bcd59a7a0b.

myth is the original or which culture got it right. It's just an interesting look at one of the aspects of tree mythology.

Middle East

In the Middle East, an area historians and cartographers used to call Asia Minor, several cultures trace the start of life to a particular tree. Quite a few of the world's current belief systems can trace at least part of their foundations to the region, which makes it a very important point of origin for this book. But before addressing this region's attachment to divine trees, a quick history lesson:

Mesopotamia was the region of Asia Minor that centered around the Tigris and Euphrates rivers. In today's geography, the region encompasses Iraq, Turkey, Kuwait, and Syria. People have been living in this area at least since 14,000 BCE. Over the centuries, different cultures held dominance and, even as they faded, influenced the cultures that succeeded them.

The first culture we have written evidence of is the Sumerian culture. Based on that evidence, it is believed the Sumerians acceded to dominance in the area beginning around 3200 BCE. This is the culture that gave us the Gilgamesh legends.

Around 2334 BCE, Sumer fell to the Akkadians. The Akkadians had been around during the Sumerian dominance but overcame that culture. Because of their exposure to Sumer, the Akkadian legends took on a very Sumerian flair.

The Akkadians didn't last nearly as long as the Sumerians before eventually falling to the Amorites, who established Babylon (after a brief intercession of the Gutians and re-emergence of the Sumerians) around 1790 BCE. The influence of the Babylonians lasted until around 1595 BCE.

What followed was a litany of conquerors from the Hittites to the Assyrians to the Persians to the Romans. But all these civilizations were heavily influenced by the Sumerians who preceded them.

Babylon

Mesopotamia was fully invested in the idea of the Sacred Tree of Life. Regardless of who was in charge, the tree image is strong in this culture. Both gods and kings are described as mighty trees.[40] In the Epic of Erra, the Babylonian god Marduk alludes to himself when he asks Erra,

> Where is the *mēsu*-wood, flesh of the gods, the proper insignia of the King of the World,
>
> The pure timber, tall youth, who is made into a lord,
>
> Whose roots thrust down into the vast ocean through a hundred miles of water to the base of Arallu [hell],
>
> Whose topknot above rests on the heaven of Anu?[41]

Erra, the god of pestilence and destruction (also known as Nergal), has decided to destroy Babylon, and he needs Marduk to go along with it or at least be out of the way in order to do that. The Epic of Erra describes the story in detail. At this point in the epic, Marduk is basically asking Erra where he gets off planning to destroy the god's city when Erra is certainly not a "pure timber, tall youth, who is made into a lord." Unfortunately for the people of Babylon, Marduk wasn't too happy with his subjects at the moment. Erra eventually

---

40. "Enki and the World Order: Translation," The Electronic Text Corpus of Sumerian Literature, Faculty of Oriental Studies, University of Oxford, last modified 2001, https://etcsl.orinst.ox.ac.uk/section1/tr113.htm.
41. Stephanie Dalley, ed. and trans., *Myths from Mesopotamia: Creation, the Flood, Gilgamesh, and Others* (New York: Oxford University Press, 1989), 291.

convinces Marduk to let him have his way—at least for a time. Babylon was toast.

Sumer

Marduk is not the only god to be compared to the Tree of Life.

The Sumerian god of wisdom, Enki, who is equated with Ea later in history, is compared to the *mes* or *mes halu-ub* tree in cuneiform tablets that have been unearthed in the region. *Mes* is translated as "sacred law." The mes halu-ub tree is also seen in folklore as the *huluppa* or huluppa tree in reference to the Gilgamesh legends. It is sometimes described by researchers as a Cosmic Tree but is better seen as a representation of the goddess Inanna. In Moyra Caldecott's telling of Inanna and the huluppa tree myth, Inanna has her brother, Gilgamesh, do a little pest control on the tree to rid it of a serpent, an abzu bird, and the dark goddess, Lilith.[42] In this myth, the huluppa tree may have been a weeping willow (*Salix babylonica*), according to Assyrian scholar Samuel Kramer.[43]

Gilgamesh does the job a bit too thoroughly. He runs off the interlopers but ends up cutting down the tree and carving a bed and throne for his sister from the wood. Hardly a fitting ending for a tree that is supposed to have generated life on Earth!

Fortunately for us, there is an alternative to the huluppa tree that also happens to be in Sumer. It is the Tree of Life located in Eridu. This was the *kiskanu* tree, one of many miraculous trees in the Grove

---

42. Moyra Caldecott, *Myths of the Sacred Tree* (Rochester, VT: Destiny Books 1993), 27.

43. Samuel Kramer, *Gilgamesh and the Ḫuluppu-Tree: A Reconstructed Sumerian Text* (Chicago: University of Chicago Press, 1938), 1.

of Eridu.[44] Eridu, according to Sumerian legend, was thought to have been at the headwaters of the Tigris and Euphrates rivers and was the first city to rise from the freshwater ocean of Apsu.

The tree is variously described as having white, black, or brown bark. It was always in fruit, always in leaf. In one translation of an old cuneiform tablet, the tree was said to have been created by Enki. He "caused it to grow in a clean place in the nether world, where it abides, in the nether world—loading it with desirable things."[45] In this context, it has the appearance of lapis lazuli with white crystal roots and grows as large as a forest, casting a huge shadow.

When parts of the tree were applied for healing, they provided "the source of life, eternal youth, and its sap flows from the deep regions of the primordial waters-abzu."[46] Even the gods used it.

Archaeologists have had a field day trying to determine if the kiskanu was a real tree. The most popular assumption is that it was a palm, although some have identified it as a cedar. This would certainly fit in with other ideas in the region. In areas of Persia (now Iraq), some researchers believe "the Tree of Life stood for the male organ and was the palm tree."[47]

44. Daniel Bodi, "The Double Current and the Tree of Healing in Ezekiel 47:1-12 in Light of Babylonian Iconography and Texts," *Die Welt Des Orients* 45, no. 1 (2015): 33–34, http://www.jstor.org/stable/43697616.

45. S. Langdon, "The Legend of the Kiskanu," *Journal of the Royal Asiatic Society of Great Britain and Ireland* 4 (1928): 844, http://www.jstor.org/stable /25221428.

46. Daniel Bodi, "The Double Current and the Tree of Healing in Ezekiel 47:1-12 in Light of Babylonian Iconography and Texts," *Die Welt Des Orients* 45, no. 1 (2015): 34, http://www.jstor.org/stable/43697616.http://www.jstor.org /stable/43697616.

47. "Genesis Myths, Mesopotamian Mythology," Circle of Ancient Iranian Studies, accessed May 23, 2022, https://www.cais-soas.com/CAIS/Religions/non -iranian/Judaism/Persian_Judaism/book4/pt7.htm.

In her book *The Assyrian Sacred Tree: A History of Interpretations*, researcher Mariana Giovino thinks the kiskanu may not have been a real tree at all or even a stylized form meant to represent a tree in a generic sense. Rather, she thinks the tree represented might have been a cult object—a thing to be honored as a representation of deity that might have taken on magickal qualities in its own right at some point.[48]

By the way, things don't end well for the earthly paradise of Eridu and the four surrounding cities. After creating mankind to serve the gods, the deities (specifically Enlil, the chief deity of the Sumerian pantheon) became upset over the constant racket humans made.

A determination was made to wipe out the noisy denizens of Eridu with a great flood. Only Ziusudra, some number of his family, and whatever animals the group could gather survived because Ziusudra secretly had been given a heads-up by Enki to build a boat.[49]

Seven days after a world-drenching flood, Ziusudra's boat grounds and the family gets out. Enki makes his subterfuge known to Enlil, Ziusudra is elevated to godhood, and humankind gets back to business. Whether folks make a pact with Enlil to be quieter this go-round or he simply resigns himself to the racket in exchange for regular worship isn't clear.

What is clear is that the original paradise garden of Eridu and the kiskanu tree are gone. The tree never returns, although the city of Eridu survives today as the modern-day site of Tell Abu Shahrain.

48. Mariana Giovino, *The Assyrian Sacred Tree: A History of Interpretations* (Fribourg, Switzerland: Academic Press Fribourg, 2007), 201.
49. Thorkild Jacobsen, "The Eridu Genesis," *Journal of Biblical Literature* 100, no. 4 (1981): 523, doi:10.2307/3266116.

Persia

Zoroastrianism developed in Persia around the fifth century BCE and was prominent in the region until around the sixth century CE. In this tradition, animal life springs from the carcass of Gavaevodata, a giant bull that is neither male nor female. Gavaevodata, the primordial bull, was created by Ahura Mazda (Ohrmazd) at the same time that he created Gayomart (also Gayomard, Gayomartan), the first man.

Ahura Mazda is the originator and source of all good in the Zoroastrian faith. He is opposed by his brother, Ahriman (Angra Mainyu), the source of darkness and chaos. After Ahura Mazda creates the universe in six stages (seven if you count the divine Amesha Spenta he created to help him), Ahriman destroys all six stages. He kills Gayomart and Gavaevodata too, for spite.

Several versions of what happens next appear. In one, Gavaevodata's seed or essence was recovered by the Moon Goddess, who cleansed it and used it to shape the first man and woman. Some versions have the next humans springing up from Gayomart's remains.

But other translations have humans coming from Gavaevodata's corpse along with all plant and animal life on Earth. Mashya, the first man, and Mashyana, the first woman, are two branches of a tree. In other translations, a tree that rises from the corpse is split in half to make the two first humans.

From these two first humans, the world is repopulated. Because they have been given free will, the battle between Ahura Mazda and Ahriman for humankind's salvation continues.

As a brief aside, it should be noted that in some translations of the Mashya and Mashyana myths, they don't start life, strictly speaking, as a tree. In this motif, they come from Gayomart's sperm after the original man was killed and his sperm has lain dormant in the ground for 40 years. And, when they do sprout, they come up as a rhubarb plant.[50] The couple is blessed by Ahura Mazda as the predecessors of human beings and told to go forth in good thought, good deed, and good word. And, oh by the way, don't be worshiping demons. Incidentally, they don't listen to any of this. They get corrupted pretty quickly by the demons.

Why is a rhubarb plant (*Rheum rhabarbarum*) picked to be a possible candidate for the "sacred tree" in this myth? This is unclear. Obviously, to those who developed the stories of the first human beings in the Middle East, rhubarb was deserving of special regard.

Israel

As other religions developed around the Fertile Crescent, researchers have made a connection between the kiskanu tree in Eridu and another famous tree or perhaps trees.

Those who have been exposed to Christian, Jewish, or Muslim traditions are likely familiar with the trees in the Garden of Eden. In Genesis 2:9, in addition to all the trees that provide food and that are pretty to look at, "the tree of life also in the midst of the garden, and the tree of knowledge of good and evil" were said to grow.[51] Some researchers believe that one or both of these trees are simply reinterpretations of the kiskanu tree.

Regardless of the connection, in the Christian paradise Adam and Eve are directly told by God in Genesis 2:17 never to eat from

50. Abass Saeedipour, "Dramatic Myths in the Avasto-Rig Vedic Pantheon: The Dramatic Myth of Mashya and Mashyana Revisited," Payame Noor University, Tehran, accessed April 14, 2021, https://www.academia.edu/32003021 /Dramatic_Myths_in_the_Avasto_Rig_Vedic_Pantheon_The_Dramatic _Myth_of_Mashya_and_Mashyana_Revisited?email_work_card=view-paper.

51. *The Holy Bible*, Holman Pronouncing Edition (Philadelphia, PA: A. J. Holman Company, 1914), 8.

the Tree of Knowledge, but they can eat freely from any other tree, presumably up to and including the Tree of Life.[52]

Oddly, for Christians the greater focus has always been on the Tree of Knowledge—specifically as it pertains to humankind's exclusion from access to it. The text seems to suggest eating to maintain eternal life is okay as long as Adam and Eve continue to be ignorant of whatever knowledge is provided by the other tree.

The Tree of Life is not mentioned again until Genesis 3:22.[53] At this point, the couple have committed the sin of disobedience by eating of the Tree of Knowledge of Good and Evil. God says knowing good and evil makes them akin to deity. To prevent Adam and Eve from eating from the Tree of Life and, therefore, living forever, God sends the couple from the garden and sets up one of the cherubim to guard the entry with a flaming sword to prevent their return.

Further references to the Tree of Life are in Proverbs, as a metaphor for wisdom, and in Revelation, where true believers are promised access to it to gain eternal life at the end of time.

Before leaving this region of the ancient world, it should also be mentioned that in a Christian context, the Tree of Life may have been an olive tree (*Olea europaea*). However, this could have been just a reliable metaphor in a region where the olive tree was seen as a very important resource. If you say, as some early Christian church leaders purportedly did, "Christ is like an olive tree," most of your Mediterranean audience is going to immediately understand you mean "a source of everlasting, life-giving energy."

---

52. *The Holy Bible*, Holman Pronouncing Edition (Philadelphia, PA: A. J. Holman Company, 1914), 8.

53. *The Holy Bible*, Holman Pronouncing Edition (Philadelphia, PA: A. J. Holman Company, 1914), 10.

It should be mentioned some consider the Jewish Sephiroth (or Sefirot) to be a Tree of Life. The Sephiroth come to us from the Jewish mystical tradition of Kabbalah. One of the original texts on Kabbalah is the *Zohar*, first published in the thirteenth century. While the oral tradition may be thousands of years old, the diagrams of the Sephiroth we know today are first seen in the sixteenth century and originate from the work of German theologians and other scholars of the time.

One of the most well-known is a diagram made up of 10 spheres arranged in three columns with 22 pathways between them (see page 130). At the top is Keter or Kether, the crown, the final step before reaching God or Ain Soph Aur. At the bottom is Malkuth, the mundane world.

The three spheres on the left column are called the pillar of severity. The three on the right are called the pillar of mercy. The center four spheres are the pillar of mildness—modern people might say synergy. These are the energies through which the Jewish God is said to have created the world. In the Jewish mystic tradition of the Kabbalah, the practitioner can meditate on these spheres and the pathways that connect them to better understand God's universe and man's relationship to it. Through this meditation, one can achieve peace and understanding.

As such, the Sephiroth are a Tree of Life in a metaphysical sense. While other Trees of Life point to a physical location for the beginning of the world and the mechanics of how it was created, the Sephiroth are the etherical emanation of the energy of the godhead figure.

From time to time, non-Jewish people become especially fascinated by Kabbalistic literature. Even our own era has seen celebrity adherents of the tradition, such as Madonna and Ashton Kutcher. It should be pointed out that the original texts were meant for Jewish people only and then only after a Jewish person had spent years studying other important religious doctrines of the faith.

Members of the Hermetic Order of the Golden Dawn and other secret societies in the nineteenth and twentieth centuries certainly were fascinated by the mysteries of Kabbalah, including the Sephiroth. Aleister Crowley wrote extensively about the tree and other Kabbalistic topics, although he spelled it *Qabalistic*, as was the style at the time. His writings were edited and presented by his assistant, Israel Regardie, in the book *777 and Other Qabalistic Writings of Aleister Crowley*. Regardie went on to develop his own interpretations in his classics *The Middle Pillar* and *A Garden of Pomegranates*. These are certainly very good resources for those wishing to explore this topic more deeply. Regardie's books, that is—not Crowley's. In my opinion, you need to be fully educated in occult philosophy, plus well-grounded and warded, before getting too deep into Crowley's teachings. Crowley had a nasty penchant for messing with people just for the hell of it, especially those whom he considered generally uninformed.

Egypt

For Egyptians, tradition offers several trees that confer life to deities, humans, or both. The sycamore is associated with Nut, seen by some as a tree goddess in addition to her association with the sky and heaven.[54] People are sustained through its life-giving waters and breath.

In other contexts, the Tree of Life was less about life on Earth and more about life in the hereafter. In the early myths, the god Re issues forth each day from behind a great sycamore tree. Since Re is

---

54. William Osborne, "The Tree of Life in Ancient Egypt and the Book of Proverbs," *Journal of Ancient Near Eastern Religions*, 14, no. 1 (2014), 114, doi:10.1163/15692124-12341259.

the source of all life on Earth, anything associated with him gains the same association.[55]

To be clear, this is *Ficus sycomorus*, or fig tree, not the sycamore maple (*Acer pseudoplatanus*) of Europe or the North American sycamore (*Platanus occidentalis*).

This has led some researchers to equate the Egyptian sycamore with the Indian banyan tree (*Ficus benghalensis*). The banyan tree is considered in many contexts to be a Tree of Life, but it has greater associations that will be discussed later in this book.

For some in Egypt's Old Kingdom (2686–2181 BCE), the way to the afterlife was detailed in the Pyramid Texts. The Pyramid Texts were truly written on the walls of a pharaoh's pyramid. For those who had access to it in the New Kingdom (1500–50 BCE), the information was written out on papyrus in *The Book of the Dead* or *The Book of Coming Forth by Day*. According to these documents, the gateway to the afterlife is between two turquoise sycamore trees. The deceased did not gain everlasting life unless he or she could pass through the gate. The lucky deceased who attained entry into the hereafter was said to have "embraced the sycamore" and "become one with the sycamore."[56]

The departed eulogizes himself upon earning this state, saying, "I clasp the sycamore tree, I myself am joined unto the sycamore tree, and its arm[s] are opened unto me graciously."[57]

According to one source, Nut steps from the sycamore tree herself to greet the departed in a garden saying, "I am Nut. I have come

55. Marie-Louise Buhl, "The Goddesses of the Egyptian Tree Cult," *Journal of Near Eastern Studies* 6, no. 2 (1947): 88, http://www.jstor.org/stable/542585.
56. Marie-Louise Buhl, "The Goddesses of the Egyptian Tree Cult," *Journal of Near Eastern Studies* 6, no. 2 (1947): 88, http://www.jstor.org/stable/542585.
57. Epiphanius Wilson, ed., *Egyptian Literature* (New York: The Co-Operative Publication Society, 1901; Project Gutenberg, 2009), 45, https://www.gutenberg.org/files/28282/28282-h/28282-h.html.

to thee bringing thee gifts. Thou sittest under me and coolest thyself under my branches.... Thy mother provides thee with life."[58] She welcomes the departed to a life of eternal bliss. To be clear, Hathor and Isis have also been described as originally being tree goddesses, but it is most often Nut who is depicted as such on tomb walls and sarcophagi.

Europe

Origin stories among European peoples, at least to the extent we know them, are less glamorous and harder to track down. These cultures weren't big on writing stuff down. As a result, what we have comes to us by way of Christian missionaries or the contacts European cultures had with Roman and Greek civilizations.

Among Nordic tribes, the first humans are formed from a couple of logs by Odin and his brothers, Vili and Ve. In other sources, the deities involved are Odin, Hoenir, and Lodur. The brothers breathed life into the logs, clothed them, named one Ask (ash tree) and the other Embla (elm tree), and created a safe space for them to live away from the Frost Giants.[59]

Why did Odin and his brothers feel the urge to whip up a human race while strolling along the beach one day? The myths we have don't say. Whether you read *Gylfaginning* or the *Voluspa* saga, barely two stanzas are given to explain the origins of humans.

Author and mythologist Henning Kure suggests that the Universe Tree known as Yggdrasil could be a metaphor for mankind.[60]

58. Alix Wilkinson, *The Garden in Ancient Egypt* (London: Rubicon Press, 1998), 99.

59. Rosalind Kerven, *Viking Myths and Sagas: Retold from Ancient Norse Texts* (New York: Chartwell Books, 2017), 26.

60. Henning Kure, "Hanging on the World Tree: Man and Cosmos in Old Norse Mythic Poetry," in *Old Norse Religion in Long-Term Perspectives: Origins, Changes, and Interactions*, ed. Anders Andrén, Kristina Jennbert, and Catharina Raudvere (Lund, Sweden: Nordic Academic Press, 2006), 68.

The first humans, Ask and Embla, were given life by the gods and a destiny by the Norns but they are more than beneficiaries of divine benevolence. They are the link between heaven and earth: "Man has his feet on the ground, anchored in this world, with roots—ties—to death and chaos in his nature. But his crown, his head or mind, is in the mental or spiritual world."[61] It is a very poetic and empowering way to look at humanity as a tree.

Celtic myths of the origins of life are even more sparse. In one interpretation of the scant material available, the goddess Eiocha is born of the sea and gives birth to Cernnunos. She procreates with him to produce other deities who eventually make humans out of oak wood.[62] The oak is also the source of all plants, meadows, and the like on Earth.

Central America

Before European influences, Central Americans venerated trees in a complex system that included trees as a source of life and rebirth. These are often presented in a directional format with, for example in Aztec traditions, the eastern tree representing the point of beginnings in Xilocochitl (a Ceiba tree) in the house of the sun god, Tonotiuh.[63] This tree was only one of four that linked to a fifth, central tree connecting not only the four cardinal directions with associated correspondences, but also the heavens, earth, and underworld.

---

61. Henning Kure, "Hanging on the World Tree: Man and Cosmos in Old Norse Mythic Poetry," in *Old Norse Religion in Long-Term Perspectives: Origins, Changes, and Interactions*, ed. Anders Andrén, Kristina Jennbert, and Catharina Raudvere (Lund, Sweden: Nordic Academic Press, 2006), 71.
62. April Holloway, "Celtic Myths of Creation," Ancient Origins, January 28, 2013, https://www.ancient-origins.net/human-origins-folklore/celtic-myths -creation-0072.
63. Felipe Solis, "Pre-Columbian Man and his Cosmos," in *The Aztec Empire* (New York: Solomon R. Guggenheim Museum, 2004), 93.

Mayans had a similar construct that included a central tree or axis mundi that incorporated four cardinal directions and a three-tiered universe of heaven, earth, and underworld. Specifically, this was thought to be the *ceiba* tree (*Ceiba pentandra*), also called Yax Che or Yax Cheel Cab in the language of the Itza Maya tribe.[64]

While these constructs include Trees of Life, the overall concept is that of a Universe Tree. Both of these concepts will be discussed later along with other myths of the Universe Tree.

North America

Populations that lived in the land mass of North America certainly held trees in high reverence. In general, their legends treat trees and other plants as imbued with individual spirits that can be contacted for advice or help.

As for a Tree of Life, I have found limited reference. In general, it appears that the stories focus on one or more creator deities who make everything from mountains to plants to people and then set the world in motion. While a story about a Universe Tree as a model for the realm of deities, the mundane world of humans, and the underworld of spirits may exist in the rich heritage of Native American legends, I have not found it.

I have found evidence of something resembling a Tree of Life. In the Iroquois myth of creation, first there is the Sky World or Upper World.[65] Below it was the dark world of water. In the center of this floating land was a large tree, covered with flowers and fruits.

---

64. Timothy Knowlton and Gabrielle Vail, "Hybrid Cosmologies in Mesoamerica: A Reevaluation of the Yax Cheel Cab, a Maya World Tree," *Ethnohistory* 57, no. 4 (Fall 2010): 709, doi:10.1215/00141801-2010-042.

65. Arthur Parker, "Certain Iroquois Tree Myths and Symbols," *American Anthropologist* 14, no. 4 (Fall 1912), 609, https://www.jstor.org/stable/659833.

At some point, the chief of the beings who lived there ordered the tree pulled up, which left a great hole. Sky Mother came to look through the hole to the space below and fell through it. She was rescued by one or more large birds (depending on who is telling the story) and carried to the surface of the water below.

The birds negotiate with a turtle to carry Sky Mother. She asks a variety of creatures to bring her some mud from deep in the water. When they do, she spreads it on the back of the turtle, which begins to increase in size, eventually forming land on which she can live. She gives birth to twins who soon create the universe and everything in it.

To be clear, several versions of this myth exist. In some cases, Sky Mother is not a deity but is simply one of the beings who live in the Upper World. The tree in the center of the world has restricted access. But Sky Mother, who is pregnant, has strange cravings and convinces her husband to bring her some roots from the tree. This creates the hole through which she falls to the darkness below. In other versions, the husband is distressed about being pressured to violate the restrictions but feels compelled to accommodate his wife. When she comes to look through the hole, it is he who pushes her out of Sky World to her fate below. As she falls, she grabs at the soil, roots, and moss in the hole and carries this down with her. Later, the woman uses the material to create an ecosystem for herself and her children.

The type of tree in the center of Upper World varies in the telling as well. Arthur Parker, a noted anthropologist of the early twentieth century and a member of the Seneca Nation of New York, determined the tree was a crab apple (*Malus*).[66] For others, it may have

---

66. Arthur Parker, "Certain Iroquois Tree Myths and Symbols," *American Anthropologist* 14, no. 4 (Fall 1912), 609, https://www.jstor.org/stable/659833.

been a balsam fir (*Abies balsamea*) or an elm (*Ulmus americana*).[67] The Iroquois Nation was large and included a number of different tribes. It stands to reason that each tribe would tend to identify with the tree that was prominent in their area.

Regardless, in the versions of the myth I can find from reputable sources, this makes the tree in question more of a Tree of Life than a Universe Tree. There is no information I can find that indicates the tree is rooted in the world that humans eventually inhabit. Also, there don't appear to be any indications that spiritual leaders used this particular tree to access other dimensions. It is an origin source and that can be enough.

Asia

In Taoist or Daoist mythology in Asia, immortality is conferred by the Queen Mother of the West, Xi Wang Mu. In Japan, she is known as Seiobo; in Korea, Seowangmo. She tends a peach orchard of 3,600 trees at the Jade Pool on the magickal mountain of Kunlun. Specifically, these are peento peaches (*Prunus persica* var. *platycarpa*), a variety originating in the wilds of China, the fruit of which is oddly flat. This shape gives the fruit its common name of "donut peach." By the way, modern mortals can test the benefits of this tree for themselves. It is available through many fruit orchard tree websites and seems to grow in most plant zones in the United States.

Xi Wang Mu's peach orchard is guarded by a nine-headed tiger to keep the unworthy at bay.[68] Every 3,000 years, principal Asian deities were invited to a banquet to partake of the fruit to insure their immortality. From time to time, Xi Wang Mu would provide

---

67. Nathan Altman, *Sacred Trees* (San Francisco, CA: Sierra Club Books, 1994), 24.
68. Jean M. James, "An Iconographic Study of Xiwangmu during the Han Dynasty," *Artibus Asiae* 55, no. 1/2 (1995): 17–41, doi:10.2307/3249761.

special humans with an elixir made from her special peaches. But these instances were few and far between.[69]

Reaching Out to the Tree of Life

Of all the trees considered in this book, the Tree of Life seems to me to offer the least by way of spiritual or ritual work. As stated in the beginning of this chapter, in so many cultures the Tree of Life is simply a story of how humans came to be. With the exception of the Abrahamic traditions, once the tree has seeded life on Earth, its job is done.

In some cases, the descendants of the Tree of Life are still with us, but like the huluppa or weeping willow, they have lost the divine spark that allowed them to create life. The same is true of the peento peaches we can find on Earth. They don't hold the same power as that of Xi Wang Mu's peach trees. In other cases, as with the kiskanu tree, it is gone, destroyed in the process of creating life.

The Trees of Life that may still exist do so far from the reaches of mortals. The Christian Tree of Life awaits those good people who are deserving in the hereafter—but that is the point. You have to be good and dead to get to it.

If stories of the Tree of Life do anything for the modern human, it may be to remind us that we all come from a common source. Our DNA is intertwined. If we can get past surface differences, perhaps we can live together as common relatives from the same origin.

Of course, doing so takes a lot of perception and insight. That's where the Trees of Wisdom come in.

---

69. Wu Mingren, "Queen Mother of the West and Her Peaches of Immortality," Ancient Origins, March 2, 2020, https://www.ancient-origins.net/human -origins-religions/queen-mother-west-0013364.

Garden of Eden

Chapter 4
Trees of Wisdom and Knowledge

Trees of Wisdom and Knowledge are different from Trees of Life. Humans are usually denied access to Trees of Life. However, they are always able to interact with Trees of Wisdom and Knowledge—if they know where to look and how to ask.

Given the long life of the largest trees in the forests of old, is it any wonder that people ascribed great knowledge to them? Trees of Life are largely mute; once you get them talking, Trees of Wisdom hardly know how to shut up. It seems, if you have had the strength and perseverance to make it to the remote reaches where the tree stands, you deserve to get the advice you seek.

In a delightful (in my opinion) scientific outcome, researchers who have long insisted that trees could in no way actually communicate are finding out different. A number of scientists have determined that trees "talk" to others in their arboreal group as well as to species of other trees. They do so, it is thought, through mycorrhizal, or fungal, networks.[70] The fungus in the soil interacts with fine, threadlike root tips of trees. What do trees talk about? They send alarms about insect infestations, disease, and growing conditions.

---

70. Ferris Jabr, "The Social Life of Trees," *New York Times Magazine*, December 2, 2020, https://www.nytimes.com/interactive/2020/12/02/magazine/tree -communication-mycorrhiza.html.

Trees also seem to share food, water, and even hormones with others in their grove. It's all part of what the researchers have dubbed "the wood-wide web." British researchers T. Helgason, T. J. Daniell, R. Husband, A. H. Fitter, and J. P. W. Young first used the term in a paper published in the journal *Nature* in 1998.[71]

To be clear, it is thought these interactions are more than just chemistry—more than a coincidence of biology. Researchers have documented instances when trees have shared resources when it might not have been in their individual interest to do so. The forest, it seems, is not a dog-eat-dog world where everyone is in it for themselves. It is a community in which the members recognize the benefits of mutual cooperation.

Even without knowing the latest research, humans have felt the community of the forest from the beginning of time. We have stories galore about trees that provided the humans who consulted them with a bounty of help. Sometimes it was advice on how to proceed in love or business. Other times, it was wisdom in general or prophecy.

Invariably, humans didn't always get the message right, especially in the case of divination. That's the problem with prophecy—even arboreal prophecy. The language is frequently laced with innuendo and riddles. If you aren't smart or wise enough to figure out the context, well, you probably weren't going to listen to the advice anyway.

Mediterranean

The Mediterranean is an area rich in history. Countries have come and gone. Their borders have changed countless times. Sometimes succeeding generations borrowed from the people who came before.

---

71. T. Helgason, T. J. Daniell, R. Husband, A. H. Fitter, and J. P. W. Young, "Ploughing up the Wood-Wide Web?," *Nature* 394 (July 30, 1998): 431, https://www.nature.com/articles/28764.pdf.

Other times, the younger generations tried to recreate the legends and myths of those ancient populations, with varying degrees of veracity. Some cultures have survived; others have faded away but still left their marks on the generations that followed them. This is certainly true when it comes to stories about the Trees of Wisdom and Knowledge.

Israel

As mentioned in the last chapter, most of those exposed to Christian, Muslim, or Jewish teachings know the story of Adam and Eve's expulsion from the Garden of Eden after eating from the Tree of Knowledge of Good and Evil. Christians most often associate this tree with the apple tree (*Malus*). That is either poetic license or a play on Latin words.

To say you want knowledge of "good and evil" is interpreted by some researchers to mean that you want to know everything—the good, the bad, and the ugly. Another explanation is that the Latin word for "evil" is *malum* while the Latin word for "apple" is *mālum*. It's the difference of a diacritical mark, in this case a macron. But scholars have only been using diacritical marks since around the fifteenth century.

Robert Appelbaum is professor emeritus of the Department of English at Uppsala University in Sweden. He traces the rationale for why we tend to link the apple tree to the Tree of Knowledge back to Pope Damasus I (305–384 CE) and the scholar and saint Jerome (342–420 CE). Damasus ordered Jerome to produce a new translation of the Bible. The result was the Vulgate translation. Appelbaum suggests in his book *Aguecheek's Beef, Belch's Hiccup, and Other Gastronomic Interjections* that prior to Jerome's translation, the word used in the Hebrew Bible of the time was *tappuach*, just a generic word for tree fruit. Jerome choose to use the Latin word, *malum*, being fully aware of the pun and that malum could be apple or evil, Appelbaum writes. Later, John Milton picked up the same pun and used it in his epic poem *Paradise Lost*. [72]

The Bible and the Torah aren't much help in identifying the tree. In both books, it is simply identified as a fruit tree. This has led religious scholars to identify it as everything from a fig to a grapefruit. While the fig is a possible candidate, the grapefruit is out of the question. Grapefruit is a natural hybrid of two other citrus trees that originated in Barbados sometime in the seventeenth century, long after the Garden of Eden was lost.

Medieval painters seem to have settled on the apple tree in their depictions of the Garden of Eden—maybe because it was familiar to them or because apples have held special places in a long list of mythologies. Regardless, they started painting Eve with an apple; the image stuck and there we have it.

They got it wrong, of course. The apple (*Malus*) didn't show up in the Mediterranean area and Middle East in general until around 2000 BC. [73] That would have been well after Adam and Eve were kicked out of the garden.

Rather than focusing on what type of tree the original writers meant, a more interesting question is, why did God forbid Adam and Eve to access a source of knowledge? And what knowledge was being denied to them?

For the average Sunday school student, the knowledge in question is the naughty stuff—sex. Adam and Eve ate the apple, immediately noticed the difference between the sexes, and were tempted to do

---

72. Robert Appelbaum, *Aguecheek's Beef, Belch's Hiccup, and Other Gastronomic Interjections* (Chicago: University of Chicago Press, 2006), 194.
73. Rebecca Rupp, "The History of the Forbidden Fruit," *National Geographic*, July 22, 2014, https://www.nationalgeographic.com/culture/food/the-plate/2014/07/22/history-of-apples/.

naughty stuff. That's why they became ashamed and tried to hide their nakedness. Up to that point, they had been wandering around the garden without a care or a stitch of clothing to their names—kind of like a carefree version of Discovery Channel's *Naked and Afraid*.

That explanation might be a bit shallow. Jewish writers have a deeper rationale. The problem wasn't so much the acquired knowledge as it was an issue of disobedience. Adam and Eve broke God's law and that had to have consequences.[74] Plus, in knowing evil, humans were not equipped to deal with the knowledge. Unlike God, they were not perfect and so would be confused and easily led into the harm of doing the wrong thing.

Another explanation might be that up until the point when the couple became aware of the possibility of evil, they were bathed in the presence of God's light. They were a part of God, knowing no other existence. When they became aware, they were no longer a part of the perfection of God. They were apart—separated from divinity. Since Adam and Eve willfully separated themselves from God spiritually, God took the next action to separate them from him physically. They were cast out. They could take their knowledge but they couldn't take immortality. From that point, humans would have to work, sweat, suffer, and sacrifice in order to earn their way back into paradise.

For adherents to Christianity, this is a very sad example of too much knowledge being a bad thing.

Greece: Dodona

Like many sacred trees in legend, the oracle trees at Dodona are oaks. Originally, the trees in Epirus, Greece, were sacred to Gaia, but over

---

74. Rav Zeev Weitman, "The Tree of Life and the Tree of Knowledge," Torah Har Etzion, March 29, 2017, https://www.etzion.org.il/en/tanakh/torah /sefer-bereishit/parashat-bereishit/bereishit-tree-knowledge-and-tree-life.

time, they became associated with Zeus. These were possibly either Kermes oaks (*Quercus coccifera*) or holm oaks (*Q. ilex*), the most prevalent oak trees on the western side of Greece.

Hesiod noted in one place in his *Theogony* that doves in the Dodona oaks gave visitors insights. At another point in his work, he says priests interpreted the rustling of the leaves of the oak trees.[75] This is echoed in the *Iliad* when Achilles invokes the image of Dodona as he asks for help from Zeus. In his adorations, he references the sacred oaks at Dodona, where "the Selli, race austere! surround, / Their feet unwash'd, their slumbers on the ground; / Who hear, from rustling oaks, thy dark decrees," and then proceeds to solicit help for Patroclus in the upcoming battles with Troy.[76] His prayers were only half answered. Later, Ulysses consults with the oracle at Dodona to advise him on how best to return to his home after the long war—in person or in disguise.

British historian Moyra Caldecott records in her book on sacred trees that at some point in antiquity two black doves flew out of Egypt. One went to Dodona and the other to Libya.[77] The one in Dodona immediately began to offer prophecies to those in attendance. Interestingly, Herodotus claimed that it was one of two women, not two doves, who was the first seer at Delphi. He claimed he was told by priests in Thebes that the women had been kidnapped from Egypt and sold—one in Dodona and the second in Libya. He said, in his opinion, the women were priestesses at a temple to

---

75. Hugh G. Evelyn-White, trans., *Hesiod, The Homeric Hymns, and Homerica*, Loeb Classical Library Volume 57 (London: William Heinemann, 1914), 215.

76. Homer, *The Iliad of Homer*, trans. Alexander Pope (London, 1899; Project Gutenberg, 2002), 295, https://www.gutenberg.org/files/6130/6130 -h/6130-h.htm.

77. Moyra Caldecott, *Myths of the Sacred Tree* (Rochester, VT: Destiny Books, 1993), 110.

Zeus in Thebes, Egypt. They were captured by Phoenician sailors and sold into slavery. Herodotus believed the locals at Dodona thought when the women spoke in their native tongue, they "seemed to utter 'bird-like noises.'"[78] That, he said, is where the legend of the black doves came from.

British author and archdruidess Jacqueline Paterson writes that the wood for the prow of Jason's ship, the Argo, came from Dodonian oak and was fitted there by Athena. When the Argonauts were in trouble, Jason could consult the oak for advice as readily as if he had attended the ritual site itself.[79] However, the Greek author Apollonius of Rhodes details in his epic poem *The Argonautica* that Athena herself had an oak beam brought from Dodona to serve a divinatory purpose for the Argo.[80] Since Apollonius is one of the most cited sources of the Argonaut myth, his report should probably take precedence.

Belief in the divine nature of the oaks at Dodona was apparent from the third century BCE until the fourth century CE when the Christian Emperor Theodosius was said to have had the last oak cut down in his drive to eradicate paganism from the lands under his control.[81]

78. D. M. Nicol, "The Oracle of Dodona," *Greece & Rome* 5, no. 2 (1958): 136, http://www.jstor.org/stable/640927.

79. Jacqueline Memory Paterson, *Tree Wisdom: The Definitive Guidebook to the Myth, Folklore and Healing Power of Trees* (San Francisco: Thorsons, 1996), 177.

80. Apollonius Rhodius, *The Argonautica*, trans. R. C. Seaton (Cambridge, MA: Harvard University Press, 1912; Project Gutenberg, 2008), bk. 1, https://www.gutenberg.org/files/830/830-h/830-h.htm.

81. Mark Cartwright, "Dodona," World History Encyclopedia, January 8, 2015, www.ancient.eu/Dodona/.

Greece: Delphi

One other famous Tree of Knowledge was a group of laurel trees at Delphi on Mount Parnassus in Greece. Like the oaks at Dodona, the laurel trees at Delphi, the location, and the chasm below the oracle site were once sacred to Gaia. Her temple was guarded by a giant serpent or python. Apollo killed the python and took possession of the site.[82] He set laurels there, according to legend, to honor Daphne, a naiad nymph who had self-dedicated to his sister Artemis, the huntress. *Daphne* is the Greek word for "laurel."

While the location was known as a religious site even in the time predating the era in which Apollo was believed to have taken over, it is his priestesses of prophecy known as the oracles with whom we associate the site. The Oracle at Delphi enjoyed a large following from roughly the eighth century BCE to the fourth century CE. Everybody who was anybody came to ask the Pythia for advice and insight.

For example, when Europa was carried away by Zeus, her father Cadmus consulted the oracle regarding her whereabouts. He didn't get an answer to that question. Instead Apollo, through his priestess, sent Cadmus to establish the city of Thebes.[83] The oracle sent Hercules off to his cousin, King Eurystheus, to do penance in the form of twelve labors for the crime of killing his family. Orestes came to ask how to lift the curse on his family's name. Many of the heroes of Greek myths consulted the oracle before starting a quest.

Beyond legend, the Roman Emperor Julian (331–363 CE) attempted in the real world of his time to reinvigorate the site, which

---

82. Jessica Mellenthin and Susan Shapiro, "The Delphic Oracle," Mythology Unbound, Utah Education Network, accessed January 9, 2021, https://uen .pressbooks.pub/mythologyunbound/chapter/the-delphic-oracle/.

83. Edith Hamilton, *Mythology: Timeless Tales of Gods and Heroes* (New York: New American Library, 1940; repr. New York: Little, Brown & Company, 1969), 254.

was losing significance in a world turning more and more to Christianity. He sent an emissary to do the work sometime during his brief reign as emperor between 360 and 363 CE, the year of his death. However, the emissary allegedly came back with the last message from the remaining spirit of the place, telling the emperor, "No longer does Phoebus [Apollo] have his chamber, no mantic laurel, nor prophetic spring; and the speaking water has been silenced."[84]

American historian Timothy Gregory casts doubt on this story as a bit of Christian propaganda. His research indicates that Julian's emissary did not find Delphi in total disrepair. Relatively underutilized perhaps, but closed? No.[85]

Sadly, while there was no Apollonian swan song or, for that matter, no violent closure of Delphi by hostile Christian forces, by the fifth century CE, the site no longer attracted suppliants looking for answers from a laurel-chewing Pythia. The Oracle at Delphi faded into history, laurel trees and all.

Persia

Alexander the Great (356–323 BCE) learned of his impending death from not one but two trees, according to the medieval manuscript *Roman d'Alexandre en prose* (*Prose Alexander Romance*). After conquering the city of Prasias, Alexander's guides told him of a magnificent place not far from the city. In this garden were the Tree of the Sun and the Tree of the Moon in the Garden of Bakalali. Like the Garden of Eden, the exact location of the garden is not known

---

84. Timothy Gregory, "Julian and the Last Oracle at Delphi," *Journal of Greek, Roman, and Byzantine Studies* 24, no. 4 (1983): 356, https://grbs.library.duke .edu/article/view/5801/5255.

85. Timothy Gregory, "Julian and the Last Oracle at Delphi," *Journal of Greek, Roman, and Byzantine Studies* 24, no. 4 (1983): 356, https://grbs.library.duke .edu/article/view/5801/5255.

but, in legend, it was believed to be in the Punjab region of western India or possibly in the eastern reaches of the Persian empire. We also can't relate the trees in this myth to any actual trees we might know today.

Alexander's guides told him that as the sun rose, traversed the sky, and set in the west, the Tree of the Sun would utter prophecies. With evening and the rising of the moon, the Tree of the Moon took over to give prophecies. Alexander described the trees as being similar to cypress and bearing fruit—the Tree of the Sun, male fruit, and the Tree of the Moon, female fruit.[86]

Having traveled far and conquered all he saw, Alexander asked the Tree of the Sun whether he would ever see his mother, Olympia, and his home of Macedonia again. The tree spoke in an Indian dialect. With much trepidation, his Indian guides translated the message and told him, "Soon you must die by the hands of your friends."

Upset by this information, Alexander decided to hang around and get a second opinion from the Tree of the Moon. The Tree of the Moon confirmed the original prophecy, saying, "King Alexander, you must die in Babylon. By your own people will you be killed and you will not be able to return to your mother Olympia."

Obviously, Alexander was distraught. He waited until sunrise and asked the Tree of the Sun if, at the very least, his body might be carried back to Macedonia. The reply was a firm no. The tree told the king this was the price he would have to pay for all of those he had killed in battle and deprived of their privilege of seeing their homes again.

"And just as one sows, so in fact shall he reap," the tree warned.

---

86. Pseudo-Callisthenes, *The Romance of Alexander the Great*, trans. Albert M. Wolohojian (New York: Columbia University Press, 1969), 129.

The prophecy continued. Not only would his body not be laid to rest in Macedonia, but his beloved mother would also die at the hands of his countrymen and his brothers would be killed by Alexander's companions. He was further advised to stop asking: "Make no more inquiries about these matters, for you will not hear more about what you ask."[87]

Alexander had to be resigned to accepting his fate. He returned to Babylon in 323 BCE, where he died. Some accounts claim he died of a fever; others detail that he was poisoned by one or more of his companions. Either way, he never made it back to Macedonia. His body was confiscated by Ptolemy, one of his generals, and taken to Egypt, where it was lost to history.

It was a sad end to a short and glorious life, but it does illustrate a serious warning to those who go seeking answers from any prophetic source. Questions you don't want to know the answer to, you really shouldn't ask.

Europe

Much of what we know of European tree legends is centered around the Celtic and Nordic tribes that inhabited the broad continent. The Celts were recognized as a large group of tribes beginning around 900 BCE, when travelers from the Mediterranean countries first took note of them. The Nordic tribes were recognized as a group with similar language and traditions around 200 CE.

---

87. Pseudo-Callisthenes, "Alexander Romance ('Pseudo-Callisthenes')," Attalus .org, trans. E. H. Haight (1955), A. M. Wojohojian (1969), and E. A. W. Budge (1889), accessed May 19, 2022, chap. 17, http://www.attalus.org /translate/alexander3b.html.

Celtic Legend

Ancient Celts reportedly had a strong attachment to their sacred trees. Stories of sacred oaks, yews, ash, apples, and hazels are attested to by Romans who encountered Celt tribes on their conquests.

The hazel has particular significance as a Tree of Knowledge. British historian Della Hooke, in her book *Trees of Anglo-Saxon England*, writes that at the source of the River Boyne in Ireland there was a mound topped by nine hazel trees sacred to the great goddess Boinn (also Boann or Boannd). These trees shed nuts into the river below, making the waters a source of wisdom. If one drank those waters in the month of June, one would become a great poet.[88]

The trees in this case were probably *Corylus avellana*, the hazel most commonly found in Ireland and Europe. However, anyone living in a temperate zone in the Northern Hemisphere can try their hand at growing a hazel tree. Several varieties grow in plant zones 4 through 9.

In the myth of Fionn mac Cumhaill, or Finn McCool, the focus is on the Salmon of Knowledge, which swam in the river and ate the hazelnuts as they fell. Finn and the legends surrounding him make up the Fenian cycle of Irish myths.[89] He and his band of warriors were believed to have lived around the third century CE and had many adventures over parts of Ireland.

But before Finn became a hero, he apprenticed himself to a druid living on the River Boyne. The druid was there to catch the Salmon of Knowledge. The salmon had come up the River Boyne as a young fish and eaten the sacred hazelnuts, thereby gaining all the knowledge of the world as well as immortality. It was said whoever could catch and eat the Salmon of Knowledge would absorb all that knowledge.

---

88. Della Hooke, *Trees in Anglo-Saxon England*, Anglo-Saxon Studies 13 (Suffolk, UK: Boydell Press, 2010), 14.
89. Iain Zaczek, *Chronicle of the Celts* (New York: Sterling, 1999), 76.

The druid eventually caught the salmon and instructed his apprentice to cook the fish while he rested. Finn was told not to eat any of the fish, even as little as a taste. The druid conveniently declined to mention the bit about acquiring the knowledge of the world. He also forgot to mention that whoever got the first taste of the fish won the divine right to complete the meal.

As luck would have it for the druid, as the fish cooked, some of its fat popped out of the fire and onto Finn's thumb. In an unthinking gesture, Finn put his thumb to his mouth and immediately began to absorb the salmon's knowledge. The druid realized what had happened and accepted it as fate. Finn was instructed to eat the remainder of the fish and so complete his destiny.

This is but one of several stories involving one hero or another eating sacred hazelnuts and going on to intellectual glory—in song, prophecy, or wisdom. Sometimes the hero gets the wisdom of the nuts after feeding on a salmon that has consumed them; other times, he eats the nuts directly.

Unlike some of the sacred trees mentioned in this book, seekers didn't always have to find one particular hazel tree. It seems groups of sacred hazel trees could be found all over Ireland and England. These were usually associated with a sacred river like the River Boyne. It should be noted that the River Shannon also had a sacred cluster of nine hazel trees that also conveyed wisdom. The headwaters of River Shannon were also stocked with salmon that feasted on the nuts.

Norse Legend

Yggdrasil is best known as the Norse Universe Tree, but it has a role to play as a Tree of Knowledge too. Odin was said to have hung on Yggdrasil for nine days until he received the knowledge of the runes. *Yggdrasil* has several interpretations, but in this instance, it is translated as "Odin's Horse." It's a fanciful play on words in which *Ygg* is another name for Odin and *drasil* is a Norse word for "horse." This could also be a grim example of medieval humor. Evidently, "horse," at one time, was slang for the gallows.

Yet another interpretation is that Yggdrasil is a horse in the sense that shamans would "ride" the tree to reach other worlds—the horse (tree) in this sense is the conduit to those places where hidden knowledge lies. Odin, being a master shaman, used Yggdrasil as his transportation to get to the place where the knowledge he sought was hidden.

To be clear, when Odin hung on Yggdrasil, he didn't get the runes directly from the tree. He either meditated on them in the pool below him or he reached into the pool to retrieve them.

Hávamál is a collection of Nordic poems, proverbs, and general guidelines for living, said by believers to have been given by Odin himself. In a translation of *Hávamál*, it would seem he quite literally reached down into the waters below to pull them out. In addition to the guidelines, it also includes Odin's description of how he acquired knowledge of the runes. In this translation of verses 137 and 138, he said:

> I trow I hung on that windy Tree
> nine whole days and nights,
> stabbed with a spear, offered to Odin,
> myself to mine own self given,
> high on that Tree of which none hath heard
> from what roots it rises to heaven.
>
> None refreshed me ever with food or drink,
> I peered right down in the deep;
> crying aloud I lifted the Runes
> then back I fell from thence.[90]

---

90. *Hávamál: The Words of Odin the High One from the Elder or Poetic Edda*, trans. Olive Bray, ed. D. L. Ashliman, University of Pittsburgh, last modified March 28, 2003, https://www.pitt.edu/~dash/havamal.html#runes.

The pool is the Well of Urd, where the Norns (sometimes referred to as the Nordic Fates) dwell, and is beneath one of the three roots of Yggdrasil. The Norns are keepers of the runes, the secret knowledge. In addition to keeping the runes, they are said to have carved runes on Yggdrasil. It's hard to know if this was done solely to protect the tree or if, by carving the runes into Yggdrasil, the tree absorbed the secret knowledge of the runes. Also, to my knowledge, there is no myth that explains where the Norns acquired knowledge of the runes.

Regardless, once he acquired the knowledge of the runes, Odin was reborn as a rune-master, charm maker, master of wind and fire, and all-around powerful magician.[91]

It should be noted that Yggdrasil is a place where knowledge can be found beyond the runes. In its topmost branches, the great eagle sees all and knows all. Yggdrasil is a conduit for information as when the squirrel, Ratatoskr, runs up and down the tree, ferrying insults between the eagle at the top and the serpent at the bottom.

In other Trees of Knowledge, the seeker obtains knowledge by speaking to the tree, holding a branch from the plant, having a tool made from the wood (wand, staff, etc.), or eating a fruit or nut from the tree. In this case, knowledge is not inherent in Yggdrasil. Because Yggdrasil is not a source of knowledge, according to legend, I believe this makes it a much better example of a Universe Tree than a Tree of Knowledge.

Getting in Touch with Trees of Wisdom

Unlike the Tree of Life, Trees of Wisdom have a very utilitarian aspect to them. Over the centuries, humans had every reason to believe, if they could get an audience with such an arboreal counselor,

---

91. Rosalind Kerven, *Viking Myths and Sagas: Retold from Ancient Norse Texts* (New York: Chartwell Books, 2017), 43.

they might receive the information they needed. It is no different for today's seeker.

Whether you find a tree in the family of wisdom trees or take an astral journey to one that is more remote, you can ask for assistance. It may be as simple as making a connection with a hazel tree or an oak in your backyard. Or you could use a guided meditation to take yourself to the Garden of Bakalali to speak with the Tree of the Sun or the Tree of the Moon.

In my experience, this takes time and patience whichever tree you decide to consult. For a long time, I had an oak in the front yard. It had been badly pruned many years prior to the time I moved to the place. I noticed that it was riddled with holes and gaps where several limbs had rotted out. The squirrels spent hours chasing one another up and down and in and out of the trunk.

One lazy summer day just as the sun was setting, I decided to see if I could use this oak as a transition point for astral travel. After warding and preparing myself, I set about meditating on the tree in front of me. I imagined myself following a squirrel into the body of the oak. We moved deeper and deeper into the trunk.

At some point, my squirrel companion left me alone in the dark, moist interior. I continued on until I seemed to see a light ahead. As I moved to it, I could see an opening. When I emerged, I was in what seemed like a watercolor painting. The general outlines of a landscape were there in soft yellow, pink, and tangerine colors. In the distance, I had the impression of people talking softly. It was almost like an Impressionist painting—a gentle place of calm and sweetness. Just standing there gave me a wonderful sense of peace.

By and by, I decided to leave. I turned back into the trunk of the tree and with very little difficulty, found my way back out. By this time, the sun had set and night had fallen.

That little trip didn't provide any great epiphany. But then, I hadn't been looking for one. On the few occasions I have taken such trips in search of information, I find it best to simply go to wherever the journey takes me and then sit, listen, and look. Sometimes, an answer presents itself during the meditation. Sometimes it doesn't. Other times, something I have seen or heard will randomly pop back into my head at a later date and I have a better understanding of what I need to do.

I don't know if it is the spirit of the tree that is communicating with me or if it is some other spiritual counselor. I am comfortable with the belief that the tree has played an important role in my quest for answers.

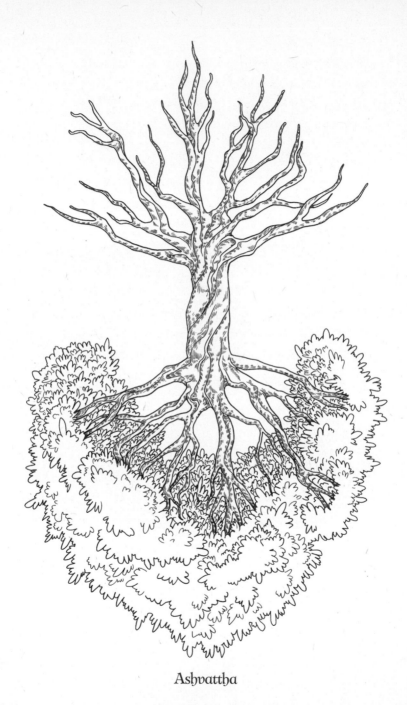

Ashvattha

Chapter 5
Universe Trees

It seems the concept of a Universe Tree is, well, universal. At some point, cultures around the world developed an understanding of the structure of the universe that was best illustrated by some form of giant tree.

Most often, it was in fact a giant tree. From the ash tree of the Norse to the ceiba tree of the Mesoamericans, models of the Universe Tree were generally based on the tallest tree in a tribe's general environment. Most often, in the real world the tree provided most of the basic necessities of life, from shelter to food. On occasion, some trees offered fragrant flowers as well.

Regardless, this is the tree in totality. No image of a Universe Tree is complete without the root system. Trees of Knowledge cast their information through their leaves or inherent spirit. No mention is made of the roots. Trees of Life provide nourishment from the ground up. Again, there is no mention of the roots.

The Universe Tree has to incorporate the top, middle, and bottom as is shown in the stories that follow. Carl Jung perhaps said it best: "No tree, it is said, can grow to heaven unless its roots reach down to hell."[92]

---

92. Carl Jung, *Aion: Researches into the Phenomenology of the Self*, vol. 9, part 2, of *Collected Works of C. G. Jung*, trans. R. F. C. Hull (Princeton, NJ: Princeton University Press, 1959), 43.

Early humans weren't selfish when it came to setting up their concept of a Universe Tree. In all the examples provided in the upcoming pages and in many of the cases not included (because there are simply too many!), early thinkers included a host of animals significant to tribal or village life.

Deer scampered about the branches, while birds, usually birds of prey, made a home there. Creatures of all sorts were either created from the Universe Tree or found a safe haven in its canopy, under its canopy, and below ground.

The tree also provided space for those who were departed. Artwork recovered in archaeological digs in Central America show trees with wide spreading branches and flocks of birds. The birds are thought to be the souls of the recently departed. If the souls were not a part of the tree, the Universe Tree provided the infrastructure to access those souls, as when Central and Eastern European shamans used the tree to find answers to pressing problems on Earth. Those shamans could also use the tree to get to demons and deities.

In the case of the Asian bodhi tree, the structure was decidedly one-way (unless you were a Buddha). Provided a person could navigate the infrastructure, at the end of the journey was enlightenment and an end to the constant cycle of rebirth back on Earth. Who wouldn't want to be free of that drudgery?

As noted repeatedly, the most well-known Universe Tree for Westerners is Yggdrasil. However, Nordic tribes didn't come up with this understanding on their own. It is believed (at least based on written records) that before there was Yggdrasil, there was the Sky-High Tree.

The Sky-High Tree

A general reverence for trees could be found throughout the area of Central Europe from Paleolithic times well into the modern era. This is the portion of the globe that is home to Slavic people in central, eastern, and southeastern Europe. Slavs are usually subdivided into those in the east, including Russians, Ukrainians, and Belorussians; those in the west, including Poles, Czechs, Slovaks, and Lusatians; and finally, those in the south of Central Europe heading toward the Mediterranean Sea—the Bosnians, Serbs, Croats, Slovenes, Macedonians, and Bulgars.

It should be pointed out that the term "Slavic" is about as exact as the term "Celtic." Both terms refer to a lot of different tribes and groups of people who spoke a related language. It doesn't mean all Slavs were united at any time in early history under one ruler. According to one researcher, "Ancestral Slavic, or Proto-Slavic, languages developed somewhere, however, and today's rough consensus is that their speakers lived, from about the second half of the first millennium BCE, somewhere in the territory of Central and Eastern Europe loosely bounded by the Dnieper (Dnipro, in Ukrainian) River basin in the east and the Vistula River basin in the west, the Carpathian Mountains and perhaps the Danube delta in the south, and the forests beyond the Pripet (Prypiat) basin in the north."[93]

While not Slavic, several other countries in the area shared a common devotion to trees including those countries we now know as Latvia, Lithuania, Hungary, and Romania.

Geographically, the home of the Slavic people is the area that bumps up against Russia to the east and Austria and Germany to the

---

93. Adrian Ivakhiv, "The Revival of Ukrainian Native Faith," in *Modern Paganism in World Cultures: Comparative Perspectives*, ed. Michael Strmiska (Santa Barbara, CA: ABC-CLIO, 2005), 211.

west. Politically, while tribes of people formed loose alliances in ancient times, there weren't countries in the sense we know them now. However, in the modern era, countries that eventually formed in Central Europe were once under the sway of various overlords through time, from Napoleon to Soviet Russia. Many won a form of independence in the twentieth century, with others still being, in varying degrees, under the influence of modern-day Russia.

From a religious standpoint, these various countries held on to their traditions until the arrival of Christianity. Christian dominance occurred at different times from the eighth to the twelfth centuries, depending on the country. Not infrequently, Christianity came at the behest of the prominent ruler of the region at the time. Eventually, as it did in so many places in the world, Christianity became recognized as the only official state religion, all the while for the most part casting a blind eye to the paralleling pagan practices going on subtly in the background. The church leaders were willing to pretend nothing was going on as old traditions and beliefs hung on.

Ukraine

Reverence for the Universe Tree was one of those old ways. For example, in Ukraine, especially in and around the Carpathian Mountains, researchers found a standard model of the Universe Tree by deciphering old poems and folk songs. We see three tiers, including the root zone, where demiurges (demons) and the souls of the departed go. The middle around the trunk was identified with the mundane world, and the top was the residence of honored deities.[94]

---

94. Tetyana Goshchytska, "The Tree Symbol in World Mythologies and the Mythology of the World Tree," *The Ethnology Notebooks* 3, no. 147 (2019): 636, https://nz.lviv.ua/en/2019-en-3-10/.

Russia

In the Russian creation myth, the universe begins as a cosmic egg. Rod, the creator god, hatches himself out of the egg. He sets to work, sorting out all the elements of the world, including oceans, stars, the sun and moon, winds and rain, and so on. In the midst of all this creating, he creates Mother Earth, who promptly dives down into the deepest ocean.

At some point, Rod creates a son named Svarog. It is Svarog who comes up with the Universe Tree in order to keep separate his father's divisions of heaven, earth, and underworld. In some versions of the myth, Svarog makes the Universe Tree from a branch taken from Mother Earth while she is still dormant under the ocean. In others, he uses some remnants of the cosmic egg.

Researcher Tetyana Goshchytska found that the symbol of the Universe Tree was even carried to the grave. She writes that in Scythian cultures, the burial mound would often be topped with a pole onto which a branch of a tree (usually oak) was attached: "This evokes associations with the tree as a memorial sign that was characteristic of the Slavic tradition."[95]

Lithuania

While the Ukrainians don't appear to have used the specific term "Sky-High Tree" to identify their concept of the Universe Tree, it can be found in the surrounding countries. References are found for the Sky-High Tree in many central European and Siberian legends. In Latvia, they speak of the *Austras Koks*, while Lithuanians call it

---

95. Tetyana Goshchytska, "The Tree Symbol in World Mythologies and the Mythology of the World Tree," *The Ethnology Notebooks* 3, no. 147 (2019): 628, https://nz.lviv.ua/en/2019-en-3-10/.

Ausros Medis or *Austras Koks*. The people in these countries used the ash or oak to symbolize their Universe Tree.

The image of the tall tree with spreading branches is found throughout Lithuanian culture. Like most Universe Trees, the top is the home of deities and the middle section under the canopy is populated by humans. In this case, the root zone gives birth to springs and pools of wisdom.[96]

In addition to carving stylized trees in home furnishings and buildings, Lithuanians still construct physical representations of the Universe Tree in the form of tall poles, capped with one or three small roofs to symbolize the three-part division of the universe.

While spiritually, Austras Koks or Ausros Medis is a means for the shaman to carry out the practical work of contacting the far reaches for answers to earthly problems, it is also a vehicle for heroes of the past to accomplish their heroic acts. One popular story involves a young and poor swine herder who must climb a magickal tree in the king's garden to figure out who is stealing the fruit. The tree in this story is an apple tree, but it still serves the function of the Universe Tree as a cosmic ladder to a spiritual realm well above where humans can see.[97] Sometimes the hero battles a dragon; other times it is a giant. But he always comes out on top with a princess bride to boot!

---

96. Vytautas Straižys and Libertas Klimka, "The Cosmology of the Ancient Balts," *Journal for the History of Astronomy*, archaeoastronomy supplement 28, no. 2 (1997): S62, https://doi.org/10.1177/002182869702802207.

97. Gyula Illyés, "The Tree that Reached the Sky—a Hungarian Folk Tale," trans. Caroline Bodóczky, *Hungarian Review* 4, no. 6 (2013): n.p., http://www .hungarianreview.com/article/20131201_the_tree_that_reached_the_sky _a_hungarian_folk_tale.

Siberia

Given the migratory habits of early humans, it's not totally surprising to find similar early religious traditions reaching eastward into Siberia.

In Siberia, the Universe Tree was known as *Tuuru* or *Turu* and was seen in the Siberian larch (*Larix decidua*). For the Siberian shaman, Tuuru was the cosmic ladder connecting heaven, earth, and the underworld.[98] It was also the nursery for the souls of shamans. Before being born on Earth, the shaman's soul would be nurtured and developed in its own special nest. The higher the nest in the tree, the stronger the shaman who is raised in it will be, the more he will know, and the further he will see. In life, the shaman's animal soul remained with the tree.

Once on Earth, the shaman would return to the tree through drumming and dance in search of answers for his people. These quests could be related to any number of needs, from health concerns to the hunt for lost livestock.

The tree of choice for the Siberian shaman was the larch. Like most of them, this earthbound representative of the Universe Tree grows to enormous heights, in this case up to 150 feet in the Northern Hemisphere. The shaman would use a young larch hung in the center of a specially built tent where workings were often done.[99] The tent opened in the east and in the west. In a dream or trance state, the shaman climbed the branches of the larch tree to access the heavens, having sent one of his spiritual helpers ahead as a scout. Interestingly, at least for the Siberian Evenk tribe, the tree to heaven

---

98. Joseph Campbell, *Primitive Mythology*, vol 1. of *The Masks of God* (New York: Penguin, 1976), 256.

99. Henry Michael, ed., *Studies in Siberian Shamanism* (Toronto: University of Toronto Press, 1963), 93.

was hung upside down because this tribe believed it was rooted in heaven. This is not unlike the concept of the Hindu and Buddhist *Ashvattha* tree, which is also upside down.

If the journey required going to the underworld, the shaman "floated" there via a larch tree with its roots pointed down. He did so from a platform in the tent surrounded by weapons and the tools of his trade. Around the inside of the tent were representations or symbols of animals that were special to the tribe, such as reindeer, stags, and salmon as well as guardian spirits and the evil spirits the shaman might be trying to banish or defeat.

Like most Universe Trees, the Tuuru knitted together three worlds—the upper world of heaven, the middle world of humans, and the underworld, occupied by spirits, good and bad.

Hungary

In Hungary, the Universe Tree had several names. It is the *Egig ero fa*, *Világfa* (World Tree) or *Tetejetlen fa* (Tree without a Top). They all translate roughly to the "Sky-High Tree." This tree united the heavens, earth, and underworld. It was a conduit along which a shaman, or *táltos*, could travel to find answers to problems or questions on Earth.[100]

❀ ❀ ❀

All the trees in these cultures are truly universal. For the true believer, it wasn't necessary to travel to a specific spot or sanctuary, although doing so might be on the adherent's bucket list. Any tree could be the connection to the one Universe Tree. Not unlike Buddhist tradition in which the divine spark is said to be in all things, so

---

100. Nóra Csécsei, "The Worldview of Hungarian Paganism," *Daily News Hungary*, May 25, 2020, https://dailynewshungary.com/the-worldview-of-hungarian-paganism/.

does the essence of the Universe Tree pervade all trees and images of trees in these traditions.

Yggdrasil

Of all the Universe Trees, Yggdrasil is perhaps best known among those who follow European traditions. It is the world ash, "the best and greatest of all trees; its branches spread over all the world and reach up above heaven."[101] Much of what we know of Yggdrasil comes from the writings of Snorri Sturluson (1179–1241), a thirteenth-century Icelandic poet and historian, particularly the *Prose Edda*, also known as the *Younger Edda*. This is different from the *Poetic Edda*, a collection of poetic narratives of unknown authorship that predate Sturluson's *Prose Edda*.

In this document, described by experts as a poetic handbook based on Norse legends as he learned them in Iceland and in his travels, Sturluson lays out the evolution, construction, and final destruction of the universe, along with all of the gods and supernatural beings in it.

Sturluson lived in Iceland from 1178–1241.[102] Unlike many of the chroniclers of ancient religious history in the past, he was no cleric. Well educated and well traveled, Sturluson was a poet, historian, and politician. It is said he compiled the *Prose Edda* to help his countrymen better understand their rich heritage. The time of pagan Norsemen had long passed even in Sturluson's time and many

---

101. Snorri Sturluson, *The Younger Edda, Also Called Snorre's Edda of the Prose Edda*, trans. Rasmus Anderson (Chicago: Griggs & Co., 1879), 72.
102. "Snorri Sturluson—A Biography," Icelandic Literature Center, accessed January 27, 2021, https://www.islit.is/en/promotion-and-translations/icelandic-literature/icelandic-titles/nr/894.

people had forgotten the old legends. Sturluson felt compelled to bring those stories back to life.

His description of Yggdrasil requires strong visualization skills because of the inordinate way in which he wrote that Yggdrasil grows. Even in his day, people had trouble understanding the allegories and poetic references of the old sagas.

In regard to Yggdrasil, Sturluson describes a massive tree with two roots spread out as we would expect them to along and underneath the ground. However, the third reaches up to the heavens to form a connection to where the gods live. Oddly, this isn't a direct route along which anyone would travel between the other worlds. That route is said to be Bifrost (Bilrost or Bivrost), a rainbow bridge between the worlds.

Perhaps it is inexact to say "anyone" would travel along Bifrost. The giants were unable to access it until Ragnarök. As for humans, well, forget about it.

But in Sturluson's description in the *Younger Edda*, he wrote that "one root is with the asas [the gods] and another with the frost-giants, where Ginungagap [Chaos] formerly was; the third reaches into Niflheim; under it is Hvergelmer, where Nidhug [a serpent dragon] gnaws the root from below."[103]

At a later point in his nineteenth-century translation of Sturluson's work, Rasmus Anderson wrote:

> **Our ancestors divided the universe into nine worlds, and these again into three groups:**
>
> **1. Over the earth. Muspelheim, Ljosalfaheim and Asaheim.**

---

103. Snorri Sturluson, *The Younger Edda, Also Called Snorre's Edda of the Prose Edda*, trans. Rasmus Anderson (Chicago: Griggs & Co., 1879), 72.

2. On the earth. Jotunheim, Midgard and Vanheim.

3. Below the earth. Svartalfaheim, Niflheim and Niflhel.[104]

In this lineup, Muspelheim is a land of fire, Ljosalfaheim is another name for the land of elves, and Asaheim is the gods' home, Asgard. On earth, Anderson places the frost giants in Jotunheim, humans in Midgard, and the second tier of Norse gods, the Vanir, in Vanheim. In the lowest regions, he has the dwarves in Svartalfaheim or Nidavellier. In this region, there is also no man's land or Niflheim and Hel's home, Niflhel. This is based on his interpretation of Sturluson's work.

These are not the only understandings of the description of Yggdrasil's layout. Joshua Mark shares a diagram by Finnur Manússon on the website Ancient History Encyclopedia. Yggdrasil's branches reach up to the heavens. The tree is supported by three roots that divide the universe of gods, humans, and other supernatural beings. One root is grounded in the place of Ginnungagap—where the universe was born out of chaos but where (prior to Ragnarök) the frost giants live. In the time of the frost giants, the land is called Jotunheim. This is also the location of Mimir's spring, where Odin goes to acquire knowledge.[105]

A second root is in Midgard, where humans live. It is connected by the Rainbow Bridge, Bifrost, to Asgard, where the gods or Aesir live.

On the level of Asgard is Alfheim, where elves live. Nearby is Vanaheim, home to the Vanir, who are gods who fought with the

---

104. Snorri Sturluson, *The Younger Edda, Also Called Snorre's Edda of the Prose Edda*, trans. Rasmus Anderson (Chicago: Griggs & Co., 1879), 259.

105. Joshua Mark, "Nine realms of Norse mythology," Ancient History Encyclopedia, December 20, 2018, https://www.ancient.eu/article/1305/nine-realms-of-norse-cosmology/.

Aesir. They lost the war but retain their godlike characteristics, second only to the Aesir. Freyr is said to rule over Alfheim, although he is a Vanir.

Below Midgard is Helheim, home to its mistress, Hel. Hel is a child of Loki, relegated to the cold, dank area by Odin, where she is overseer to all of the souls that don't make it to Valhalla. Also below Midgard is the realm of the dwarves, Nidavellier or Svartalfheim. Not far away is Niflheim, a cold, misty land where no one and nothing lives.

The fate of the dearly departed is varied in Norse legend. Warriors and select princes went to *Valhöll* (Valhalla), situated in the top of Yggdrasil, according to twentieth-century folklorist H. R. Ellis Davidson.[106] Davidson was a British scholar who specialized in the study of Celtic and Germanic religion and folklore. She also noted that those who could afford it constructed large grave mounds where they were buried along with a variety of housewares, weapons, and food. From there, these ancestors could keep watch over their descendants or be contacted for advice.

The rest of the population—the old, the sick, the dishonored—went to join Hel at Helheim. The journey was hard, through biting cold winds and pitch black darkness. Those who made it arrived at Nastrond, the shore of corpses. Modern Norse Pagan Ryan Smith says that some could go no further. Referencing the *Völuspá*, he says that perjurers, murderers, and men who seduced the wives of others fall prey to Nidhug.[107] This is the serpent who relentlessly gnaws at

---

106. H. R. Ellis Davidson, *The Road to Hel: A Study of the Conception of the Dead in Old Norse Literature* (London: Cambridge Press, 1968), 96.

107. Ryan Smith, *The Way of Fire and Ice: The Living Tradition of Norse Paganism* (Woodbury, MN: Llewellyn Publications, 2019), 107.

the base of Yggdrasil—when it isn't noshing on those so damned even Hel won't have anything to do with them.

Beyond Nastrond is a hall with a roof of poisonous serpents that drip venom and the Echoing Bridge. No human condemned to this region leaves. Any attempt to cross the Echoing Bridge brings a challenge from Hel's assistant, the giantess Modgudh. The entrance to Nastrond, called Gnipahellir, is guarded by a nasty mutt named Garm, who performs a service similar to Cerberus, the Greek canine guardian of Hades.

As my grandmother used to tell us children when we worried about those things that go bump in the night, "Them that's dead and gone to heaven don't want to come back. Them that's dead and gone to hell can't come back." In the case of the Norse Helheim, this is true until Ragnarök, when Hel and her lifeless horde will rise from Helheim. Accompanying her to fight the Aesir will be her father Loki onboard Naglfar, a grisly ship made of the toenails and fingernails of the dead.

On that dismal note, it is time to point out that Yggdrasil isn't all doom and gloom. There are rays of sunlight, even in the cold Scandinavian countryside. And there are entities of good purpose too.

Yggdrasil's universe is populated by a number of supernatural entities like the Norns, three lovely ladies named Urd (the past), Verdandi (the present), and Skuld (the future). Like the Fates in Greek mythology, the Norns know the past, present, and future. They can be consulted by the gods for insight, but they can't be petitioned by gods or humans to change what was, is, or will be.

The Norns sprinkle water on the Universe Tree and patch its roots with clay to overcome the damage done by Nidhug, who gnaws constantly on the tree's roots. As a brief aside, some sources give *Jormungand* as the name of the dragon that gnaws at the roots of Yggdrasil. They are two different creatures. Jormungand is the world serpent that encircles Midgard, not the root-eating serpent dragon under Yggdrasil.

At the top of the tree is an all-knowing eagle, according to Sturluson. Between his eyes sits a hawk.[108] Why, Sturluson doesn't really say.

Four stags leap among the branches of Yggdrasil while a nasty, troublemaking squirrel called Ratatoskr scampers up and down the tree, carrying malicious gossip and insults between Nidhug and the eagle. Again, we don't know why. Historian J. H. Philpot, writing in her book *The Sacred Tree* in 1897, suggested the animals in Yggdrasil's branches are metaphors for meteorological forces: "The stags who bite the buds are the four cardinal winds; the eagle and the hawk represent respectively the air and the wind-still ether; the serpent Nidhug who gnaws the root in the subterranean abyss symbolises volcanic forces, and the squirrel, who runs up and down the tree, hail and other atmospheric phenomena." [109]

And why not? Why shouldn't these creatures be metaphors for environmental forces? Sturluson was trying to capture his nation's history in myth but he, like many other historians of his time and since, may have been less than true to the original myth. He has been criticized for "Christianizing" the myths and legends he recorded. Given that he was writing down myths in the thirteenth century that were developed hundreds of years earlier, he could hardly be blamed for misunderstanding the intent of the original storytellers. It should also be borne in mind that Sturluson wasn't writing necessarily for

---

108. Snorri Sturluson, *The Younger Edda*, trans. Rasmus B. Anderson (Chicago: Scott, Foresman & Company, 1901; Project Gutenberg, 2006), 74, https://www.sacred-texts.com/neu/pre/pre05.htm.

109. J. H. Philpot, *The Sacred Tree: or, The Tree in Religion and Myth* (London: Macmillan, 1897; Project Gutenberg, 2014), 115. https://www.gutenberg.org/files/47215/47215-h/47215-h.htm.

historical accuracy. His agenda was national identity or, rather, the promotion of a national identity.

We do know that other historians recorded the presence of a mundane representation of Yggdrasil at Uppsala, Sweden. Writing in the eleventh century, the Catholic monk Adam of Bremen recorded the existence of a great temple at Uppsala. The building was surrounded by a gold chain and roofed in gold. Outside stood an evergreen tree. Was this a worldly Yggdrasil? We don't know. However, it is certain that the locals venerated the place and honored Thor, Freyr, and Odin there with sacrifices and rituals.[110]

What is a bit clearer is that ancestors of the Vikings Sturluson spoke with in Iceland and Norway may have assimilated some of the ideas about their Universe Tree from populations they encountered on their way north and later in their raids into Southeast Europe and nearby Siberia.[111] For example, the similarities between the Siberian Tuuru, Hungarian Egig Ero Fa, and Nordic Yggdrasil are striking.

The Slavs even have a version of the world serpent. In their creation myth, Svarog moves the winds and waters to raise Mother Earth from below the ocean and keeps her afloat on the giant serpent, Yusha. When Yusha wiggles, the earth quakes.[112]

110. Wu Mingren, "The Royal Mounds of Gamla Uppsala," Ancient Origins, October 11, 2018, https://www.ancient-origins.net/news-ancient -places-europe/royal-mounds-gamla-uppsala-ancient-pagan-site-sweden -002866.

111. Ingrid P. Nuse, "First Scandinavians Came from North and South," Science Nordic, January 12, 2018, https://sciencenordic.com/archaeology -forskningno-society-culture/first-scandinavians-came-from-north-and -south/1453083.

112. Janey, "Slavic Creation Myth: Translated from 'Songs of the Bird Gamayan,'" College Russian, September 12, 2008, https://collegerussian.com/2008/09 /12/slavic-creation-myth-translated-from-songs-of-the-bird-gamayun/.

Evocations of the Universe Tree can be seen as far away from Scandinavia as the Pacific coast, where Korean kings of the fifth to sixth century CE wore gilded crowns with outlines of a scaffolded, three-tiered tree that looks remarkably like the modern-day Romuva tree symbol (see also page 115).

Romuva

What Yggdrasil meant to the ancients who viewed it as a description of the universe seems to be simply that—Yggdrasil is and was a model of the universe. Humans don't meditate on Yggdrasil any more than they might meditate on a map of the world.

Humans don't travel to find Yggdrasil. They live on it. Interestingly, the average human doesn't really seem to travel anywhere outside his or her part of Yggdrasil, although the gods certainly do.

Humans definitely didn't wander up to Asgard. Heimdall, one of Odin's sons, is the gatekeeper who keeps out humans and giants. Humans also would not have wanted to wander down to Helheim. It surely wasn't as fun as Valhalla, so why seek to go there? Better to live a good life in Midgard, fight the good fight if the opportunity presents itself, and pray to Odin and your ancestors for a ticket to Valhalla.

Tɦe Upside-Down Tree

Some 4,000 miles away in India, the notion of a Universe Tree takes an interesting turn—quite literally. The Ashvattha tree has its roots in heaven and its canopy on Earth. In this case, the tree is the sacred fig, important to both Hindus and Buddhists. It is the *Ficus religiosa* mentioned in the earlier discussion of Trees of Life.

English anthropologist E. O. James suggested that Indo-Europeans found a flourishing devotion to sacred trees when they invaded the Indus Valley and Punjab regions of India in the second century BCE.[113] Temples complete with altars would be set up under a sacred peepal (also pipal) tree that was believed to ensure life and fertility. The peepal tree is the *F. religiosa* tree.

Like many sacred trees, the peepal tree is tall, reaching close to 100 feet in maturity. It is also very long-lived, living anywhere from 900 to 1,500 years when not damaged. Occasionally, a few have survived even longer. The Jaya Sri Maha Bodhi in Sri Lanka is thought to be over 2,000 years old. Tradition has it that the tree was planted in 288 BCE and rooted from a cutting from the original tree under which Buddha received enlightenment.

In times of famine, people harvested figs from the tree. The figs of the peepal tree aren't especially tasty, so they would usually be reserved for animals. People could not have helped but notice that the tree survives in the harshest of weather and soil conditions. Food, shelter, resiliency—what more could you ask of a sacred tree?

This was the attitude about trees that invaders encountered when they arrived so long ago. Early Indo-Europeans came out of the area of Central Europe in the Caspian Sea region. Why they came boiling out of this area to have a significant impact on the language

---

113. E. O. James, *The Tree of Life: An Archaeological Study* (Leiden, Netherlands: Brill, 1966), 147.

and culture of people from Ireland to Iberia to India is uncertain. However, based on a study of language and archaeological artifacts, researchers are reasonably certain that, in India, the Vedic tradition and later Brahmanism were greatly influenced by multiple waves of invaders from Central Europe.

Specifically, researchers see their impact in the Vedic hymns developed not long after those initial waves started. This isn't to say India owes its religious tradition to Central Europe. Far from it. Cultural historian Dr. Thomas Berry wrote that the Indo-Europeans or Aryans found a flourishing religious tradition as they arrived around 2000 BCE. In his book *Religions of India*, he said that the development of Hinduism was the result of an "Indianization of non-Aryan traditions." Berry continued, "By Indianization is meant that the non-Aryan native elements gradually modified the Aryan elements and, over the centuries, achieved an ever-larger place in the total pattern of cultural and spiritual interaction."[114]

These traditions, beliefs, and mythologies are explained in many documents, including the Vedic Hymns (*Rig-Veda*, *Sama-Veda*, *Yajur-Veda*, and *Atharva-Veda*), the Upanishads, and the Bhagavad Gita. These documents describe the important Indian deities, methods of sacrifice and honoring, the order of the universe, the meaning of existence, and all the major tenets of Hinduism.

The Ashvattha tree is mentioned in the Hindu document *Katha Upanishad*. In part 2, chapter 3, verse 1, we find the classic description of "that eternal Ashvattha tree with its root above and branches

---

114. Thomas Berry, *Religions of India* (Chambersburg, PA: Anima Publications, 1992), 19.

below. That root, indeed, is called the Bright; That is Brahman (the eternal truth) and That alone is the Immortal."[115]

All worlds are contained there and nothing exists beyond it. According to James, the Ashvattha tree is ever renewing and sustaining all life. It is the "manifestation of Brahman in the cosmos."[116]

In Hindu theology, *Brahman* is all things and no thing. Brahman is in all people—people without Brahman do not exist. Although texts frequently refer to Brahman as "he," Brahman is gender neutral. The ultimate goal of the *atman* (true self) is to lose the transitory husk of temporal existence and be reabsorbed by Brahman, the one true reality.[117]

The Buddhist concept of Brahman or, as that tradition expresses it, *Brahma*, is a bit different. In that theology, Brahma is a god—high up in the echelon of deities but not the absolute reality. The absolute reality is *Dharmakaya*. It is defined in the same way as Brahman in Hindu tradition—that point from which all reality comes and to which, ultimately, all would like to return.

These different interpretations of divinity and the hereafter are a bit beyond the scope of this book. The point of both Hindu and Buddhist teachings is to get back to that ultimate state of bliss that is the reunion of human and the Divine, regardless of how each defines the Divine. Both traditions prescribe several ways to do this and both make reference to a Universe Tree.

In Buddhism, the Gautama Buddha achieves enlightenment under the bodhi tree. In this case, *bodhi* translates to "enlightenment."

---

115. *Katha Upanishad*, trans. Swami Nikhilananda, Arsha Bodha Center, accessed June 1, 2022, https://arshabodha.org.

116. E. O. James, *The Tree of Life: An Archaeological Study* (Leiden, Netherlands: Brill, 1966), 152.

117. Thomas Berry, *Religions of India* (Chambersburg, PA: Anima Publications, 1992), 24.

The bodhi tree might be *Ficus religiosa* or possibly *F. indica*. Regardless, it is a sacred fig tree. Making a pilgrimage to a descendant tree of the original bodhi tree that the Buddha sat under is a key goal of many of his adherents.

The original bodhi tree is thought to have been in Bodh Gaya, Bihar, India. It was cut down several times over thousands of years, according to legend, but always miraculously regrew. The tree is also said to have been replaced a few times by cuttings from other sacred figs that were themselves cuttings of the original tree.

The story of the sacred fig begins, as Joseph Campbell explains so well in his book *Transformation of Myths Through Time*, with Siddhartha as he is called before becoming Buddha. Siddhartha was born to high station but gave up that station to find the meaning of life. He comes to the bodhi tree in the center of the universe after many attempts to find enlightenment through many other paths.[118] He sits down under the tree and declares he will not move until he finds the enlightenment he seeks. In some sources, Siddhartha sits in one spot for a full seven weeks. In others, he walks back and forth around the bodhi tree in deep contemplation over the course of seven weeks.

He is tempted repeatedly by the Hindu god, Kamadeva, god of worldly desire. When temptations of the flesh fail, Kamadeva tries fear of the death, as in "Do you really want to die like this? Because you know that's what's going to happen."

When that doesn't move Siddhartha, Kamadeva tries to guilt him with the burden of social obligation. He argues that Siddhartha has a mandate to care for people around him and fulfill the societal duties of his station.

---

118. Joseph Campbell, *Transformations of Myth Through Time* (New York: Harper & Row, 1990), 116.

None of these tactics work. In the end, Kamadeva is defeated and Siddhartha becomes the Buddha, the Enlightened One. However, instead of remaining detached in nirvana, that state of eternal bliss, the Buddha returns to the mundane world in *bodhicitta*, a state of awakened mind, as a bodhisattva in order to help others to reach the enlightened state of the Buddha.

In Hinduism, it is Brahman who convinces the Buddha to return to humanity to teach as many as will accept the knowledge how to attain enlightenment. At first, the Buddha resists. "Enlightenment can't be taught," he tells Brahman. It can only be experienced, and each individual human will have his or her own unique experience. Instead, Buddha proposes to teach the path to enlightenment. The rest would have to be up to the individual.

In the Buddhist and Hindu myths of the Universe Tree, the bodhi tree was physically at Bodh Gaya. However, Campbell explained that, in reality, the bodhi tree at the center of the universe is the ultimate unmovable spot. That spot can be anywhere. It is more a state of mind than an actual place.[119]

Your bodhi tree could be the maple in your front yard or the oak in the local park or the crepe myrtle at grandma's house. It is wherever you decide to become unmovable in your desire to rid yourself of self. To do this, you must acknowledge that life is suffering. There is a cause for suffering. There can be an end to suffering. There is a path away from suffering if only you decide to take it. These are the four truths of Buddhism.[120]

---

119. Joseph Campbell, *Transformations of Myth Through Time* (New York: Harper & Row, 1990), 116.
120. Mark Siderits, "Buddha," Stanford Encyclopedia of Philosophy, ed. Edward N. Zalta, last modified February 14, 2019, https://plato.stanford.edu /archives/spr2019/entries/buddha.

In modern language, these ideas can be summed up as follows. Life is a bitch and then you die—over and over and over again. Suffering exists in the form of daily frustration, actual pain, and more—but nobody, including any aspect of the Divine, requires you to suffer. You can stop it. Learn to see the world via meditation and studied insight as it really is, and then let it go.

For Hindus, in the Bhagavad Gita, the Hindu god Lord Krishna tells the adherent that the real sacred tree is unknowable until humans reject all passion (desire) and ignorance and achieve purity. They must chop through what they perceive as tangible (the branches of the tree) with "the sharp axe of non-attachment."[121]

Hinduism predates Buddhism and retains many of the understandings of the Indian pantheon. While adopting some of the concepts of Buddhism, Hinduism keeps the basic understandings of that tradition. As such, Ashvattha is also seen as the place where the Hindu pantheon meets. In some of the religious texts, various gods actually live in the tree roots, fruit, and leaves. In still other texts, it is the god Brahman who lives in the root of the tree, while Vishnu can be found in the middle and Shiva in the canopy. In the Hindu tradition, Brahman is the god who created all things. Vishnu is the protector and preserver of the universe. Shiva is the destroyer of all things, a step that is necessary for all things to be recreated. The three deities are frequently referred to as the Hindu triumvirate.

In this philosophy, the theme of constant reincarnation is present, but people can escape the cycle. They don't have to want to—it's an option. Hopefully, to make each reincarnation a good or better one, the adherent will live a responsible life in this existence of good

---

121. *The Bhagavad Gita*, trans. Shri Purohit Swami, HolyBooks.com, May 21, 2010, 15, https://holybooks.com/bhagavad-gita-three-modern-translations/.

deeds and productivity based on guidance in the various Vedas or sacred texts.

The Hindu who wishes to break out of the cycle of reincarnation does so by "chopping" through the branches of the Ashvattha tree that represent attachment to the mundane world. While the success of anyone doing this is contingent in part on their actions in past lives (over which one obviously has no control in this life), it is possible through good deeds, devotion to deity, and renunciation of the "fires" or passions of everyday life to achieve *moksha*, the Hindu term for nirvana.

It should be noted that the sacred fig of these traditions is truly a metaphor for a metaphysical Universe Tree. Other than using it to help adherents understand their position in the world (or how to get out of the world), it doesn't seem to hold quite the significance of the Sky-High Tree or Yggdrasil. And that's okay.

It is interesting to note that the tree connecting humans to heaven in the ancient world isn't as exotic to Westerners as it might seem—at least to those Westerners who are familiar with the writings of Plato.

Teaching roughly 5,000 miles away and 80-some years later, Plato compared humans to trees with their minds rooted in heaven and bodies bound up on Earth—an *arbor inversa*. In *Timaeus*, Plato explains that the Divine gave each person a soul located in the top of his body (head), and "the divine power suspended the head and root of us from that place where the generation of the soul first began, and thus made the whole body upright."[122]

Just like in the Asian traditions, Plato argues that when people are caught up in the mundane world, chasing earthly desires, they are doomed to a mortal death with no lingering impact. However, if

---

122. Plato, *Timaeus*, trans. Benjamin Jowett (New York: Macmillan, 1949), 73.

a person seeks knowledge, in this case, *logos*, and wisdom, or *sophia*, "in so far as human nature is capable of sharing in immortality, he must altogether be immortal; and since he is ever cherishing the divine power, and has the divinity within him in perfect order, he will be perfectly happy."[123]

This isn't to suggest that Plato was directly influenced by Eastern philosophies. As best we can tell, he never traveled beyond Greece, Italy, and Egypt. Of course these countries were visited by a lot of different travelers who carried with them knowledge from around the Eurasian continent. Maybe there was contact—maybe not. Who knows?

However, as we have seen from the discussions so far, the concept of the tree as a very handy metaphor is wide-ranging. I wouldn't argue that Plato was aware of Buddhism or Hinduism. I prefer to think that all great minds know a good idea when it occurs to them.

Universe Trees of the New World

On the other side of the globe, certain Central American cultures had their own concepts of the Universe Tree. These people lived in central and southern parts of Mexico, as well as the nations of Guatemala, Belize, El Salvador, and some portions of Honduras, Nicaragua, and Costa Rica. Many different tribes and traditions existed in the Americas, but the Maya and Aztecs are perhaps the best known.

To be clear, what we know of the mythologies of this region comes from many different sources representing the ideas of many different tribes of people. It is no more appropriate to speak of the "Maya" or the "Aztecs" as a single cohesive group than it is to talk about the Celts as one single cohesive group. Certainly, there were

---

123. Plato, *Timaeus*, trans. Benjamin Jowett (New York: Macmillan, 1949), 73.

some cultural exchanges, some borrowing and amending of traditions between peoples. That is not to say that some of the versions of the myth of the Universe Tree presented here represent the hardcore beliefs of every single person who lived in the region at any given time. Some did believe. Some believed in something kind of similar. Others would have had no idea what I am talking about.

Additionally, like some of the old European traditions, much of what we know is heavily influenced by the European conquerors and religious authorities who came in the 1500s and later. The sacred Maya text *Popol Vuh* appears to have been. It was an oral tradition prior to being written down by Spanish clerics in the sixteenth century and more fully documented in the eighteenth century by Dominican friar Francisco Ximénez. *The Books of Chilam Balam*, the last Maya prophet, certainly were interpreted by Christianity when they were committed to paper in the sixteenth and seventeenth centuries.

As is often repeated in historical research, those who win the wars write the history. In the case of religion, Catholic clerics and other religious authorities in the New World did make an attempt to understand what the tribes overwhelmingly believed—if only to understand what they were wiping out before they wiped it out. It is ironic to think, for example, sixteenth-century Bishop Diego de Landa would take the time to record the Maya writing system before overseeing the destruction of many of their books, what are called the Maya codices. But that's what happened.

Regardless, before the Europeans arrived and beginning somewhere around the second century BCE, the people in this area settled down to a largely agrarian society structure. Like their early pagan European counterparts, the tribes worshipped a number of nature deities.

For these two mega-cultures, the Universe Tree was the ceiba tree (*Ceiba pentandra*) or Yax Che Tree, the First Tree. Yax Che is one of several names given to the tree. It is a natural selection. The ceiba tree can grow in the tropic region to a monstrous 200 feet or more in height. The huge roots that brace the tree in the first few decades of its life frequently stand as tall as a person, looking quite like the flying buttresses on a Gothic cathedral.

It has a broad, spreading canopy that flowers once a year with fragrant blossoms. The fiber produced by the seedpods is useful in textiles, giving it the common name of silk-cotton tree. The seeds are expressed for an oil that is used in soapmaking and, in modern times, a petroleum oil alternative. The trunk was used to build canoes. Not surprisingly, the bark yields an additive that is used in Central and South American spiritual healing rituals.

In pre-Columbian Central America for many cultures, the World Tree connected all four directions in addition to connecting the heavens with Earth and the underworld. Many cultures in Mesoamerica saw the world as a horizontal plain divided into directional quadrants, each ruled by specific deities.[124] The center tree that kept the sky and earth separated was also called *Wakah-Chan*.

Maya

Based on studies of hieroglyphic inscriptions and sixteenth-century highland Maya texts, researcher Allen Christenson said Mesoamerican cultures through their myths describe a great tree set up at the beginning of this cycle of time to be a world axis: "In its fruit-laden

---

124. Felipe Solis, "Precolumbian Man and His Cosmos," in *The Aztec Empire* (New York: Solomon R. Guggenheim Museum, 2004), 93.

form, it personified the god of creation who fathered the progenitors of the Maya royal dynasty."[125]

Prior to this time, the earth and the heavens were pancaked together in one layer. No light was available. This was the time of the Lying-Down-Sky.[126] By the way, this is also the time of the fourth creation of the world. There had been three earlier creations that involved the emanation of deities and a couple of failed attempts to create worthy subjects to worship and honor the deities.

In one version of this story, the Maya maize god Hun-Nal-Ye separates the earth and sky and places the ceiba tree to hold the two dimensions apart. This is the Raised-Up-Sky, or the Wakah-Chan. The top of this world axis is at Polaris, the North Star.[127] When Hun-Nal-Ye set the tree in this location, he also set the celestial bodies and stars spinning about Polaris. In some interpretations, the Milky Way shares the name Wakah-Chan with the tree. The Milky Way is, in fact, the canopy of the Universe Tree.[128]

But to get back to Earth, around Wakah-Chan in four directions, with east being the primary direction, are four other trees. In some stories, these are four more ceiba trees of varying colors.[129] Specifically,

---

125. Allen J. Christenson, "The Sacred Tree of the Ancient Maya," *Journal of Book of Mormon Studies* 6, no. 1 (1997): 1, https://archive.bookofmormoncentral.org/sites/default/files/archive-files/pdf/christenson/2016-09-13/allen_j._christenson_the_sacred_tree_of_the_ancient_maya_1997.pdf.

126. Martin Brennan, *The Hidden Maya* (Santa Fe, NM: Bear and Company Publishing, 1998), 81.

127. David Freidel, Linda Schele, and Joy Parker, *Maya Cosmos: Three Thousand Years on the Shaman's Path* (New York: William Morrow and Company, 1993), 73.

128. David Freidel, Linda Schele, and Joy Parker, *Maya Cosmos: Three Thousand Years on the Shaman's Path* (New York: William Morrow and Company, 1993), 115.

129. *The Book of Chilam Balam of Chumayel*, trans. Ralph L. Roys (Washington, DC: Carnegie Institution, 1933), 100.

the tree is red in the east, white in the north, black in the west, and yellow in the south. Each quadrant has a corresponding ruling deity.

The sacred ceiba tree serves the additional function of connecting heaven, Earth, and the underworld. It arises from the back of a huge creature on land that is totally surrounded by a vast body of water.

In the Maya legends as in the Aztec versions, there were up to thirteen layers to heaven, one to earth, and nine to the underworld.[130] Each level was ruled by a specific deity. In fact, each quadrant in the mundane world also had multiple lesser deities who ruled over various aspects of weather and nature. The universe as a whole was presided over by a supreme deity who was both Father and Mother.

As in European and Siberian cultures, the tree was a conduit for access to the deities and to ancestors. A complex organization of ritual observations based on an amazingly detailed set of calendars and astronomical observations helped hold the society together under the authority of a king. Kings identified themselves as the physical embodiment of the Universe Tree. "The king was this axis and pivot made flesh. He was the Tree of Life," according to researchers Linda Schele and David Freidel.[131] Researcher Allen Christenson explains, "By portraying themselves wearing tokens of the world tree, rulers declared themselves to be the intermediaries between worlds at the center point of creation."[132]

---

130. Karl Taube, "Aztec Religion: Creation, Sacrifice, and Renewal," in *The Aztec Empire* (New York: Solomon R. Guggenheim Museum, 2004), 170.

131. Linda Schele and David A. Freidel, *A Forest of Kings: The Untold Story of the Ancient Maya* (New York: William Morrow and Company, 1990), 90.

132. Allen J. Christenson, "The Sacred Tree of the Ancient Maya," *Journal of Book of Mormon Studies* 6, no. 1 (1997): 20, https://archive.bookofmormoncentral .org/sites/default/files/archive-files/pdf/christenson/2016-09-13/allen_j ._christenson_the_sacred_tree_of_the_ancient_maya_1997.pdf.

Christenson records that one Maya king in particular, Lord Hanab-Pakal II, who ruled in the seventh century CE, had an impressive representation of the sacred ceiba tree carved into the lid of his sarcophagus in the Temple of the Inscriptions at Palenque, Mexico.[133] The tree is represented in cross form with symbols all around it indicating it glowed.

The Universe Tree in Mesoamerica was often presented in a cross form. No doubt, that made it easier for New World religious authorities to convert some Native Americans in the region by telling them their Universe Tree cross was actually the Cross of the Crucifixion.

Aztec

The Maya culture was prominent in the area of the Yucatán Peninsula roughly from 2600 BCE until 900 CE, when it was gradually overwhelmed by the Toltec culture. These people were in turn overwhelmed by the Aztec culture by the thirteenth century CE and the center of gravity, so to speak, shifted from the Yucatán Peninsula to the Valley of Mexico. The Aztecs absorbed much of the religious structure of the Maya, adding some of their own prominent deities.

They modified the world creation myth by having two deities, Tezcatlipoca and Quetzalcoatl, tear apart the giant monster of Maya myth into two halves. One half became the earth, and the other, the sky. Perhaps by coincidence or universal synchronicity, this sounds a lot like the legend of Marduk and Tiamat. In that legend from Babylon, after a mighty battle, Marduk defeats the goddess of chaos, Tiamat, and then tears her body in two pieces to make the earth and the heavens.

---

133. Allen J. Christenson, "The Sacred Tree of the Ancient Maya," *Journal of Book of Mormon Studies* 6, no. 1 (1997): 8, https://archive.bookofmormoncentral .org/sites/default/files/archive-files/pdf/christenson/2016-09-13/allen_j ._christenson_the_sacred_tree_of_the_ancient_maya_1997.pdf.

Central Mexican and Babylonian cultures are separated by 2,000 years and over 7,000 miles but, as Joseph Campbell and other researchers have frequently pointed out, there is an omnipresence to mythology that defies place and time.

Meanwhile, back in Central America, the Aztec gods were busy organizing their corner of the world. When we left them, Tezcatlipoca and Quetzalcoatl were hard at work using monster bits to make a new world. They retained the Universe Tree with three main levels:

> **The uppermost was the sky, composed of thirteen levels occupied by particular gods and celestial phenomena, including the sun, stars, and wind. The brilliant, celestial paradise of the sun, Tonatiuh Ilhuican, was the afterlife abode of valiant warriors and women who died in childbirth. The lowest realm of the universe was the nine-leveled underworld, Mictlan, ruled by the crafty death god, Mictlantecuhtli, and his consort, Mictlan-cihuatl. Unfortunate souls who succumbed to sickness or old age went to this dark and dusty region, from which there was no return.** [134]

Again, this is one version of what happened to the souls of people who died in Central America. In Maya traditions, those who died after a simple, inglorious life ended up in *Xibalba*. It was a miserable place of torture and privation. It took a long time to get there but at least, if you were clever enough, you stood a chance of outwitting the Maya death deities and ending up in one of the lower versions of heaven. That apparently wasn't an option for the deceased Aztecs.

---

134. Karl Taube, "Aztec Religion: Creation, Sacrifice, and Renewal," in *The Aztec Empire* (New York: Solomon R. Guggenheim Museum, 2004), 170.

Just as the Egyptians had instructions for the deceased in a Book of the Dead, Aztec priests offered instructions to the deceased on what to expect in the hereafter.[135] These were written down on bark paper and burned or buried with the deceased. He or she would pass between two mountains and continue past a large snake and then a huge green lizard. Next the deceased traveled through eight plateaus and eight mountain passes. The journey continued through a knife-edged wind and across a raging river. And they were still not at the entry to the underworld.

At this point, the deceased encounters Mictlantecuhtli, with whom they must negotiate passage to the nine levels of the under-world, using information from the papers sent along with him or her. It took four years to complete the negotiation to gain access to those nine levels. Once through the nine levels, the deceased must cross another river before reaching a place called *Chiconaumictlan*, where they achieved a final death. That's it. No enlightenment. No final par-adisical reward. Just gone to a world of eternal darkness.[136]

This is another key difference between the Maya and Aztec here-afters. The inglorious among the Aztecs were gone after a period of time. The Maya could and did still petition their ancestors, who tended to hang around a while longer.

On the upper end of the Universe Tree, there were thirteen levels with evocative names like the Place of Duality and Heaven That Is

---

135. Felipe Solis, "Precolumbian Man and His Cosmos," in *The Aztec Empire* (New York: Solomon R. Guggenheim Museum, 2004), 90.

136. Gabriela Bautista, Jose Jimenez, and Berna Canales, "The Human Body in Mesoamerican Ritual: Bones, Symbols and the Underworld," in *Rituals, Past, Present and Future Perspectives*, ed. Edward Bailey (Hauppauge, NY: Nova Science, 2017), 76.

Green.[137] Available information is scant about who gets into any of these thirteen levels, but it appears admittance was relatively limited.

The heavens along the Universe Tree were a place through which the sun, moon, and other celestial bodies traveled. The uppermost levels were the abodes of the deities, where they constantly died and were reborn. As for human souls (other than the majority that ended up in the underworld), they could go to one of three places.[138]

Children who died while still very young would go to *Chichihuacuauhco*, the Orchard of the Gods. Here, the innocent and pure would be fed from wet-nurse trees that provided plenty of milk, and the gods protected their little souls.

Soldiers and women who died in childbirth went to *Tonatiuh-Ilhuicac*, the Heaven of the Sun. In a rather enlightened mindset, Aztec people equated the rigors of childbirth to that of doing battle. Valiant mothers who died while giving birth deserved the honor of a warrior. In this case, those who made it to this level could join the sun on its journey around the cosmos. In four years' time, the men would become birds and butterflies while the women would evolve into domestic goddesses of spinning and weaving.

People who died by drowning went to *Tlalocan*, where they became the chosen ones of the rain god Tlaloc. Unlike many deceased among the Aztecs, the bodies of drowning victims were not cremated but buried. In this state, they feed the local vegetation and eventually produced rain that supported the earth.

---

137. Allen J. Christenson, "The Sacred Tree of the Ancient Maya," *Journal of Book of Mormon Studies* 6, no. 1 (1997): 94, https://archive.bookofmormoncentral .org/sites/default/files/archive-files/pdf/christenson/2016-09-13/allen_j ._christenson_the_sacred_tree_of_the_ancient_maya_1997.pdf.

138. Manuel Aguilar-Moreno, *Handbook to Life in the Aztec World* (New York: Facts on File, 2006), 188.

The Aztec were dominant in Central America until the arrival of the Spanish in 1517. In a few short years, the Europeans conquered the native tribes through the introduction of non-native diseases, trickery, and an advantage in military hardware. To be fair, the Spanish succeeded in part by taking advantage of fractures that already existed among tribes in the Aztec empire.

Some of the people who arrived from Europe included Catholic clerics. While many of these people took time to record much of what they saw and heard about the native culture, they also did a very thorough job of wiping out much of the recorded history of the tribes. The European invaders were so successful in destroying the native culture that it wasn't until the 1950s that archaeologists and researchers were able to begin reconstructing pre-Columbian history from the natives' standpoint. I am old enough to remember history classes in which instructors insisted that no written language existed in the pre-Columbian New World until the arrival of Europeans. How wrong those instructors turned out to be!

Yuri Knorosov, a Russian linguist, epigrapher, and ethnographer working from 1952 onward, was able to figure out the basis of Mayan language using documents recorded by the sixteenth-century bishop of Yucatán, Diego de Landa. The bishop recorded what he thought was the Maya alphabet. It turned out to be, according to Knorosov, a record of syllables that could be combined to make words.[139] Others have built on Knorosov's work over the past decades to help bring much of the old cultures back to life.

---

139. "Mesoamerican Religions: Pre-Columbian Religions," Encyclopedia.com, last modified 2019, https://www.encyclopedia.com/environment /encyclopedias-almanacs-transcripts-and-maps/mesoamerican-religion -pre-columbian-religions.

In the meantime, the native populations appear not to have forgotten the old Universe Tree structure. Just like in Central Europe, the motif was and still is popular in art, murals, textiles, sculptures, and more.

It seems however many times the Universe Tree is chopped down, it finds the energy to survive and regenerate.

Reaching Out to the Universe Tree

In this chapter, we have covered a number of Universe Trees from many cultures. However, they all share the same purpose—they give us a means to connect with divine and ancestral sources when we need guidance in life.

Much like the example I used in the previous chapter, you can use any of these motifs of the Universe Tree that speak to you to do self-guided meditations to seek help.

I don't advise wandering willy-nilly around the astral landscape provided by the Universe Tree. Preparation and safeguards are important. The astral plane is inhabited by entities of all sorts, according to current and historical experts. These include low-level thought forms, spirits of those who have not completed their journey to their next level of enlightenment, angels, and demons. Some of these entities may be helpful; others could not care less about earthly visitors. Still others are said to be perfectly willing to screw around with whomever they encounter. Ideally, you should find a trusted mentor who can help you as you encounter these entities and guide you back to the mundane world, if necessary.

If you don't have a mentor, begin your journey by first clearly determining what you are seeking. Take some time to write out what help you hope to get. Focus on one goal at a time. Wandering around this territory with a laundry list of needs may leave you confused when you return. Start your astral journey with one query only. There will be time in the future to return with new questions later. After you are done, analyze the insight you received on the one question you asked. Be patient. Sometimes the meaning isn't immediately apparent, but it should make sense to you in time.

Before doing the work, ward yourself in whatever manner your tradition advises. In my case, I would cast a circle and call guardians. In preparation, it is advised to use appropriate incense and ask your ancestors or patron deities to watch over you. When the journey is over and you leave the spiritual plane, be certain to thank whoever or whatever attempted to help, whether you understood what was presented or not. By all means, when you leave the area, mentally close the door or opening you used to access the tree in the first place. Back in the mundane world, while still in the circle, take time to have some sort of food and drink. This is called grounding. It is meant to reorient you to the mundane world.

Finally, as a word of caution, I advise people not to try to live in this other world. From time to time, I have encountered those who were so afraid of the mundane world that they tried to spend as much time as possible outside of it. In this case, I'm not talking about using mind-altering substances. These people could not seem to take a step or make a decision without attempting to consult a spirit guide or go on a journeying quest.

If you are spending all your time asking for advice and not acting on it, the advice isn't doing you any good. The journeys we can take to access the Universe Tree or any spiritual plane can be good for us, but they are meant to augment the life we live on this plane, not replace it. You will be on the spiritual plane soon enough. Learn to exist on this one while you are here.

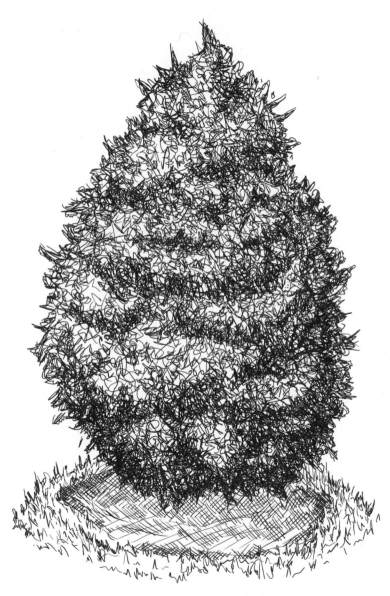

Arborvitae

Chapter 6
Modern Concepts of the Universe Tree

W hile the Universe Tree was a common concept in most early civilizations, the advent of Abrahamic traditions gradually pushed it underground or into the background of most communities. The Universe Tree and tree spirits in general faded from popular culture.

Waves of Transition

In certain instances recorded in history, Christian authorities used the cross of Christ's crucifixion as a replacement for the Universe Tree or the Tree of Life among pagan populations they encountered.

These weren't spur-of-the-moment allegories. It seems the tradition of comparing the Universe Tree to either Christ or Christ on the cross dates back to early Christianity, when church fathers made reference to the *arbor crucis* or the *arbor vitae*.[140] Arbor vitae is

---

140. Fallon, Nicole, "The Cross as Tree: The Wood-of-the-Cross Legends in Middle English and Latin Texts in Medieval England," Department of the Centre for Medieval Studies, University of Toronto, Canada, 2009, 139, https://tspace.library.utoronto.ca/bitstream/1807/19188/1/Fallon_Nicole_A_200911_PhD_thesis.pdf.

a reference to the Latin for "tree of life" in this case, not arborvitae, the common name for the landscape species *Thuja*.

Christian authorities as early as the second century CE used the term *arbor crucis* to explain to potential converts that Jesus's cross and the sacrifice it represented was a connection between heaven and earth, just like their Universe Tree. Of course, as was pointed out earlier, a true Universe Tree also must include the underworld, and the arbor crucis doesn't seem to do that.

The greater significance for Christian missionaries seemed to be to use the pagans' acceptance of a tree symbol or cross symbol to make their own doctrines more acceptable to the population. That's a reasonable argument to make and one a great number of pagans accepted. It wasn't like their lot was going to improve in this life, given the rigid social structure of the time that mandated you stayed in your own economic group regardless of how wretched life there might be. If the argument was presented with food and a new suit of clothing at your baptism or at the point of a spear, arrow, or, later, musket, then it was just so much more compelling.

For the most part, these early discussions of the nature of the cross of the crucifixion were kept mostly among the learned few. The newer traditions did retain many of the metaphors for Trees of Wisdom and of Eternal Life in their sermons to the masses, but they rejected the idea of a literal tree structure that connected the heavens, Earth, and underworld.

Humans were stuck on Earth until they shuffled off this mortal coil, and then it was up to a paternal god to determine where they ended up. A direct connection between the three spheres of heaven, Earth, and the underworld was not only rejected, but it was adamantly denied. And woe be to those who tried to communicate with anyone or anything in either of those otherworldly spheres. That was to be left to religious authorities, sometimes on pain of death, at least in the Mediterranean and Western civilizations.

This was pretty much the state of things through the fall of the Roman Empire, through the Dark Ages, and into the Renaissance. Unfortunately for the three dominant traditions that felled paganism, the Age of Enlightenment arrived with a growing suspicion and outright disregard for religion of any sort. Religious leaders who from roughly 400 to 1700 CE in the post–Roman Empire world could largely dictate human behavior began to find themselves discounted or ignored.

The Age of Reason arrived in the late 1700s. In the United States, students are taught to mark its arrival with the publication of Thomas Paine's book of the same name in 1794. Actually, it was published in three parts in 1794, 1795, and 1807. However, the movement had already begun in Europe with the rise of the deist. A deist was someone who professed a belief in the laws of nature—not Demeter's laws and certainly not God's laws but the rules that could be tested in a laboratory and certified as correct or incorrect.

Scientific thinking began to take hold, and science had a penchant for questioning everything. Soon after the questioning came the ridiculing. The world was not the center of the universe under the parental gaze of a stern father to the exclusion of everything else and neither, for that matter, was humankind.

Philosophers like Rene Descartes (1596–1650) struggled to reconcile what the church said with what scientific observation clearly denied. When his work *Discourse on the Method* was published in 1637, it caused such a stir that Descartes was forced to defend it against charges of atheism by philosophers and university heads in multiple countries.[141] The book embraced the application of reason to all things except God. God was a necessary component of all things in the world and beyond denial, according to Descartes. Regardless, his writings had the effect of giving rise to Cartesianism (knowledge as derived from sensory experience) and that angered church leaders to no end. They were ready to disown and expel him, much to Descartes's dismay. He maintained he was a devout Catholic to his dying day.

Still, as the Romantic period arrived toward the beginning of the nineteenth century and unrest was everywhere, pews began to empty out. By this time, philosopher Immanuel Kant (1724–1804) and others openly argued against the existence of god—not just the Christian God but gods in general.

It is true that during the Romantic period, artists, poets, and writers fell back in love with nature and its associated deities. Poet Lord Byron (1788–1824) mourned the death of "Mighty Pan," and painters like Eugene Delacroix (1798–1863) rediscovered the symbolism of much of the Greek and Roman deities and nature. Their influence was short lived. In no time, the Industrial Revolution reinforced the dominance of science, and for a time, there was no turning back. Well into the twentieth century, science and invention would save humankind. Nature and deity were no longer needed.

Until they were.

Science can be brutal in its assessment of life. People might welcome the advances provided by science, but they also craved the reassurance that spirituality provides. They found it in the reemergence of secret societies.

---

141. Russell Shorto, *Descartes' Bones* (New York: Doubleday Publishing Group, 2008), 27.

The time of secret societies happens in the late nineteenth and early twentieth centuries. Of course, secret societies had existed for millennia, but there was a mania for them in this time period. Organizations like the Hermetic Order of the Golden Dawn, the Theosophical Society, the Order of the Rosy Cross, and many more were formed to explore the ancient mysteries that were being rediscovered in archeological digs and the catacombs of old libraries. While many included elements of alchemy, the original science of the Middle Ages, others sought to resurrect the old gods along with what were perceived as simpler ideas like the Universe Tree model of the cosmos.

The nineteenth century also brought with it a rise in spiritualism. Spiritualism is, at its core, a belief that spirits exist and they have no reason not to talk to the living, if invited to do so. Occasionally, they do so uninvited too. Researcher Kenneth Pimple suggests it was an effort among some in the public to reconcile an ever more scientific, unimpassioned world with religion.[142]

Whatever the basis for the revival, spiritualism was eyed suspiciously by some of the upper echelons of the major religions but embraced by the congregation. Ladies of the church could attend services on Sunday morning and host sessions with a medium at their homes on Sunday evenings without fear of risking their immortal souls. After all, they were simply reaching out to the dearly departed. What could go wrong?

People scoffed, of course. Harry Houdini and P. T. Barnum were big detractors. Houdini went so far as to employ a number of secret undercover agents to help him debunk the popular mystics and

---

142. Kenneth D. Pimple, "Ghosts, Spirits, and Scholars: The Origins of Modern Spiritualism," in *Out of the Ordinary: Folklore and the Supernatural*, ed. Walker Barbara (Boulder: University Press of Colorado, 1995), 83.

spiritualists that he actively sought out.[143] But the practice had its celebrity endorsers as well, such as Sir Arthur Conan Doyle.

The modern age of spiritualism in America is thought to have run roughly from the 1840s up to about the 1950s.[144] That may have given just enough cover to allow for reemergence of interest in the old ways.

Anthropologist Margaret Murray (1863–1963) wrote *The Witch Cult in Western Europe* in 1921, but she had been advocating the notion of the dominance of a goddess-centric religion among ancient civilizations for years prior to that. She reinforced the idea with her 1933 book, *The God of the Witches*.

Others were rediscovering and exploring the old ways and gradually coming out in the open with their views. This set the stage for the likes of Gerald Gardner, arguably the father of modern Pagan practices in the major industrial countries, to begin to promote a return to pagan practices.

But neither Murray nor Gardner nor much of anyone else, for that matter, spent much time talking about the Universe Tree. As mentioned earlier in this book, the term *World Tree* didn't become a part of the common vernacular until historian Mercia Eliade (1907–1986) popularized it in the 1950s.

---

143. Gavin Edwards, "Overlooked No More: Rose Mackenberg, Houdini's Secret 'Ghost-Buster,'" *New York Times*, December 6, 2019, https://www.nytimes.com/2019/12/06/obituaries/rose-mackenberg-overlooked.html.

144. Kenneth D. Pimple, "Ghosts, Spirits, and Scholars: The Origins of Modern Spiritualism," in *Out of the Ordinary: Folklore and the Supernatural*, ed. Walker Barbara (Boulder: University Press of Colorado, 1995), 83.

Rediscovery

As the 1950s flowed into the 1960s and '70s, the Pagan movement shared a stage with the modern environmental movement. What better symbol is there for an environmental movement than a tree? The association was mutually beneficial. Chas Clifton writes in his 2013 history of American Paganism, *Her Hidden Children: The Rise of Wicca and Paganism in America*, that the rise of environmentalism in the 1970s helped move Wicca from a mystery religion to a nature religion. After all, who should care more about nature and the environment than people who regularly worship nature deities in a natural setting?

North America and England

It fell to the new Pagans to figure out how to incorporate the Universe Tree back into the generalized Paganism they inherited from Gardner and his offshoots. Reverence for trees was a given.

Margot Adler interviewed Oberon Zell-Ravenhart in 1986 for her landmark book *Drawing Down the Moon: Witches, Druids, Goddess-Worshippers and Other Pagans in America*. In the interview, he likened paganism to a tree that grows and changes through time. "And when, after many thousands of years, perhaps (for many trees are potentially immortal, never dying of old age), it should come to the end of its time, it does not pass from the world entirely, for its own progeny have, in the interval, begun to spring up all around, again from the Earth, and again, similar yet each unique. A world of Pagan religions is like a forest," he said in the interview.[145]

---

145. Margot Adler, *Drawing Down the Moon: Witches Druids, Goddess-Worshippers and Other Pagans in America* (New York: Viking Press, 1979), 24.

Some practitioners rediscovered the Universe Tree of the shaman. Writing in 1984, Selena Fox, cofounder of the Circle Sanctuary in Wisconsin, said she feels she is a channel between the earth and heaven when she practices her faith. She wrote, "I become the World tree when I Shamanize, linking the transforming Dark of the Underworld with the Awakening Light of the Upperworld."[146] Fox wrote at the time that she was not trying to re-create the shamanism of the Old World. She was trying to blend what she had learned in her studies with the realities of the modern world to find a way to make the practice relevant for Pagans of today.

It is this notion of practitioner as living conduit that Starhawk advocates in *The Earth Path: Ground Your Spirit in the Rhythm of Nature*. Starhawk is an American activist who has been an inspiration for a focus on the Goddess traditions. She is the author of the popular book *The Spiral Dance*, among other influential books on modern Paganism.

In *The Earth Path*, Starhawk advises the reader to take the pattern of the tree for grounding. The practitioner grounds energy by putting down roots into the earth. They move energy up from the earth and out into the universe through the top of their head. She writes, "The two-way flow of the branching pattern lets us draw earth energies up and move sky energies down, simultaneously. When we are rooted and grounded in the earth, any energetic lightning bolts we encounter will sink harmlessly into the earth and not burn us out. And we are linked to a source of virtually endless vitality."[147]

---

146. Selena Fox, "Wiccan Shamanism," in *Circle Network News* (Mt. Horeb, WI: Circle Sanctuary, 1984; Internet Sacred Text Archive, 1999), https://www.sacred-texts.com/bos/bos046.htm.

147. Starhawk, *The Earth Path: Grounding Your Spirit in the Rhythm of Nature* (New York: Harper San Francisco, 2005), 190.

Starhawk's book has plenty of information on working with all the elements. However, in the section on earth, she offers an excellent meditation for one or more people to connect to the universe as a tree element. It is the Universe Tree as the World Web.

Some have argued that environmentalism itself is the new religion. Roger Gottlieb is professor of philosophy at Worcester Polytechnic Institute. He has written or contributed to many books of political philosophy, environmental ethics, religious environmentalism, and contemporary spirituality. Gottlieb describes religious environmentalism as an orthodoxy that honors all of nature, including the beliefs of Indigenous peoples.[148] He advocates for an active role for participants to work toward better, sounder ecological outcomes in all walks of life. He also points out that this reverence crosses religious boundaries. In other words, you don't have to give up a Christian faith structure (for example) to embrace environmental religiosity. God wants you to protect his creation, just as Yahweh does and Allah does and Cernunnos does and the Great Spirit does and on and on.

These are just some of the ways Pagans in North America have addressed the return to the Universe Tree. The way back wasn't limited to North America and England, however.

Central/Eastern Europe

Many in the Baltic region that comprises Latvia and Lithuania have revived their spiritual past in the form of *Romuva*, a reconstruction of the region's old religion, Universe Tree and all. This is not unlike efforts of Nordic and Celtic descendants who have tried

---

148. Roger Gottlieb, "Revisited: The Case for Religious Environmentalism," The Imminent Frame, January 13, 2021, https://tif.ssrc.org/2021/01/13/revisited-the-case-of-religious-environmentalism/.

to reconstruct their own religious traditions. As in many countries, Christian elements gained dominance in the Baltic countries eventually but did so much later than in neighboring countries. For example, Nordic traditions were most fully suppressed or subverted by around the ninth century CE but in this area of Central Europe, that didn't happen until the eighteenth century CE.

Romuva is one of the Pagan traditions trying to reestablish itself in the modern era. The word means "sanctuary" or "temple."[149] The sacred fire is a key element of the tradition. According to ECER, adherents of Romuva worship "one supreme reality, which encompasses the worlds of the living and of the dead, the family and tribe, including all ancestors, all of nature, and the universe."[150]

To be fair, some would insist that the old ways never left. Although dominated by Christian and political elements, quite a few citizens in the area maintained significant aspects of the religious culture of their ancestors.

As part of their identity, adherents have reclaimed Austras Koks with a stylized symbol of the oak as their Universe Tree. This is a three-tiered scaffold topped with a sacred flame to represent the world of the dead (the past), the world of today (the present), and the world yet to come (the future).[151]

---

149. Michael Strmiska, "The Music of the Past in Modern Baltic Paganism," *Nova Religio: The Journal of Alternative and Emergent Religions* 8, no. 3 (2005): 40, https://doi.org/10.1525/nr.2005.8.3.39.

150. Jonas Trinjunas, "Lithuanian Baltic Religion Romuva," ECER, accessed June 21, 2022, https://ecer-org.eu/organisations/lithuanian-baltic-religion-romuva/.

151. "Romuva," SymbolDictionary.net, accessed January 27, 2021, http://symbol dictionary.net/?p=814.

In 2019, the Lithuanian government, or Seimas, voted narrowly to deny recognition of the religious organization. In a case ("Romuva" v. Lithuania, 48329/19) brought before the European Court of Human Rights (ECHR) in June 2021, the court ruled that the Seimas was in violation for failure to recognize Romuva without justification.[152] The court has no authority to enforce its decisions, but those decisions do carry a lot of weight in the global community.

This is all part of a larger Native Faith movement of Central and Eastern Europe. Countries across the region from Ukraine to Norway where ideas of the Universe Tree were once prominent are experiencing a public interest in reclaiming the old traditions. This is not to suggest a wholesale conversion of populations back to pagan practices. It should also be noted that the interest in the old ways coincides with a resurgence in nationalism as well. Still, the phenomenon is apparent enough to warrant a number of recent studies on the potential impact of Neopaganism on geopolitical struggles in the area.

Iceland

Iceland made news in 2015 when members of *Ásatrúarfélagið*, the Ásatrú Society (or Fellowship), announced plans to build the first temple to their Nordic faith that had been constructed on the island in over 1,000 years.

The Ásatrú Society was officially recognized as a religion in the country in 1972 by the country's Ministry of Religious Affairs. The society professes an open-minded pantheistic theology with a heavy focus on environmentalism. According to the society's website, while

---

152. "2021 Index to the Information Notes on the Court's Case-Law," European Court of Human Rights, 2022, 29, https://www.echr.coe.int/Documents /CLIN_INDEX_2021_ENG.pdf.

membership is open to any faith, instruction is provided in Nordic traditions and mythology based on the Edda poems and Snorri Sturluson's works. Obviously, Yggdrasil would be a significant feature in that instruction.

The society started out with roughly 100 members back in the 1970s and has since reportedly grown to over 4,000 in a country with a population of 356,991 in 2019.

A national promotional site estimates the majority of Icelanders identify as Christian: "Most Icelanders (80%) are members of the Lutheran State Church. Another 5% are registered in other Christian denominations, including the Free Church of Iceland and the Roman Catholic Church." About five percent of the population identifies as Ásatrú.[153] By comparison, the number of self-identified Pagans in the United States ranges from as low as 750,000 to as high as 10 million. That works out to anywhere between 0.2 percent to 3 percent of the US population.[154]

Community acceptance didn't exactly follow. The group had to lobby for the right to perform Pagan rites at Þingvellir (Thingvellir) National Park in 2000. Þingvellir was the site of the country's government, or Alþingi, from 930 to 1272 CE and is held in high regard by its citizens. The opposition to the Ásatrú Society holding Pagan observations there came from Iceland's National Church.[155]

---

153. "Quick Facts," Visit Iceland, accessed June 2, 2022, https://www.iceland.is /the-big-picture/quick-facts.

154. "How Many Pagans Are There?," Patheos, accessed June 1, 2021, https:// www.patheos.com/library/answers-to-frequently-asked-religion-questions /how-many-pagans-are-there.

155. Michael Strmiska, "Asatru (Iceland)," World Religions and Spirituality Project, August 5, 2020, https://wrldrels.org/2020/08/02/asatru-iceland/.

Even with a stubborn insistence on recognition, the construction of the tradition's temple hasn't been easy. Iceland, like much of the world, was impacted by the recession that hit in 2009. This put the development of the building on hold. Matters were complicated again by cost overruns and by the global pandemic that exploded in 2020 and continued into 2021. The latest word as this book is being written is that the temple will open soon.

World Tree

Chapter 7

The Trees We
See around Us

If the information in the previous chapters has inspired you to reach out to trees, their energies, and their accompanying spirits, you might be asking how to start. Can you grow your own Yggdrasil if you follow a Heathen's path? If you follow a Greek or Roman tradition, can you grow your own Dodona oak? Can you just find a tree with which you can connect and imagine it as your own personal understanding of the Universe Tree? Wouldn't that be a nice way to bring what you've learned so far home?

The answer to these questions is a qualified "maybe." Most of the trees described here are easy to find in the average American neighborhood. Most can be planted in the continental United States if none exist in your immediate landscape. A few can't—for a variety of reasons.

For example, the Tree of the Sun and the Tree of the Moon described in the chapter on Trees of Wisdom don't seem to have really existed. You'll come about as close to finding one of them as you might to finding a Huorn.

Others might be hard to grow outside their natural habitat. The ceiba tree of Central and South America grows in plant zones 10 to 12. If you live in a tropical area, you're in luck. If not, you'll have to set your sights on a different tree.

The same is true to a limited degree of the larch (*Larix*). The Siberian larch (*L. sibirica*), favored by shamans of that area, grows in zones 2 to 3; other larches, like the American larch (*L. laricina*), struggle in zone 5 and wither away below that range.

With other trees mentioned in legend, we once again have to hedge our bets. As an example, if you believe the biblical Tree of Life was an apple, you're in luck. Apples grow all over the Northern Hemisphere in many plant zones. If you think the Tree of Life was an olive (*Olea europaea*) or a palm tree (*Chamaerops*), you'll either have to live in or move to an area included in plant zones 10 to 12. Or you could try growing either of these inside assuming you have space available.

Fortunately, in the list of trees that follows, most are readily available either in the natural environment or as a landscape specimen. With that in mind, it's time to look at trees in our regular spiritual practice. Trees are like any herb that we use in our daily rituals and magickal practices. They have correspondences that make them appropriate resources.

Gathering your own material for spiritual work is something that can bring you more in tune with the world around you. The more you interact with the world around you, the better you understand and relate to it, in my opinion.

But before you can gather plant material from the legally accessible space in your environment, you have to know how to identify it. This may seem a small task. Who doesn't know what an oak tree looks like or a pine tree or a maple? Most of us see some species of all these every day on the way to work or while out shopping.

But there are those plants that can trip us up. Just because a tree has scaly foliage on it, does that mean it's a cedar? Or is it a *Chamaecyparis*? When is a poplar really a poplar? When is it a tulip tree and when is it quaking aspen?

Then there are the questions about seedpods versus cones versus samara. All of this can get very confusing.

The information in this section isn't meant to be a rehash of a high school biology class. It's just meant to give a few guidelines on the terms commonly used to identify parts of trees in order to make your future research a little easier.

This information is readily available at state cooperative extension offices and websites. The US Forest Service offers good identification guidelines too, as do organizations like the Arbor Day Foundation and the Audubon Society. I have relied on all these resources to help shape the very basic definitions that follow.

Before we get to tree terminology, it will be important to know the nomenclature for plants. This will prevent confusion as you do future research. The appendix covers over 20 common and well-known trees in detail, describing basic characteristics, general history, and some appropriate uses of the plant material for ritual or magickal work. In addition to the common names of the tree, I've included the Latin names. This is the only way to ensure we are all on the same page. If I say "*Liriodendron*," we will know I am talking about the tulip poplar, not the quaking aspen, or *Populus*.

Scientists aren't certain, but there may be as many as 100,000 tree species in the world. Plants that share common characteristics are assigned a genus and a species name. The species name is often descriptive, as, for example, *Juniperus communis. Juniperus* is the genus and *communis* is a Latin word for "common," meaning it is found in many places around the world.

This is the binomial Linnaean system, named after Carl von Linne, who came up with the system. Beyond that, plants may have a varietal name. These are usually cultivated plants or plants that someone has brought into existence by purposefully crossing one plant with another. An example would be the Foster holly or *Ilex ×attenuata* 'Foster', a cross between *I. cassine* and *I. opaca*.

Researchers often recategorize plants as methods and tools improve. When that happens, sometimes plants get moved from one classification to another. This happens most often when scientists get down to a detailed analysis of the plant's genome. For example, the silk floss tree was at one time categorized as *Chorisia speciosa*. After studying the tree, researchers decided it was closely related to the ceiba tree family. Its name was changed to *Ceiba speciosa*, making this a relative of the Central American Universe Tree discussed in a previous chapter.

Here's another quick clarification. When is a tree a tree as opposed to a very large shrub? What exactly is a tree?

The US Forest Service points out there really isn't a hard-and-fast definition of what a tree is. However, a generally accepted definition is "a woody plant usually having one or more perennial stems, a more or less definitely formed crown of foliage, and a height of [at] least 12 feet at maturity."[156]

Landscapers and horticulturists fidget with this in day-to-day work. For example, *Camellia japonica* is generally considered to be a large shrub that can get as much as 30 feet tall. When it is left full to the ground, it is still considered a shrub. When it is limbed up to expose a multi-stem trunk, it is considered a small tree.

This is not something to worry about. The trees discussed in this book fit well within the accepted definition of a woody perennial, usually with a single trunk and a minimum height of 15 feet at maturity.

---

156. "Definition of Terms," US Forest Service, accessed January 3, 2023, https://www.fs.usda.gov/srsfia/php/tpo_2009/tpo_docs/DEFINITIONS.htm.

Common Tree Terms

As you begin to learn more about the trees around you, you will encounter some common terms. Some are fairly obvious. Who doesn't know that the outer covering of a tree is its bark? But you may not be familiar with certain other terms, the knowledge of which could come in handy when you go out to gather resources. If you are looking for a walnut tree, for example, it helps to know that it has a compound leaf structure to narrow down your search.

Bark: The tree's protection from the outside world. The outer bark is constantly renewed from the inside. The inner bark is the pipeline through which food is passed to the rest of the tree. It lives for only a short time, then dies and turns to cork to become part of the protective outer bark.

Broadleaf: A tree with leaves that are flat and thin and generally shed annually.

Canopy: The uppermost layer in a forest, formed collectively by tree crowns.

Compound Leaf: A leaf with more than one blade. All blades are attached to a single leaf stem. Where the leaf stem attaches to the twig, there is a bud.

Conifer: A cone-bearing tree with needles, such as pine, hemlock, cedar, and fir.

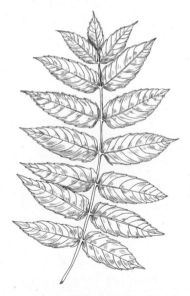

Serrated Pinnate Compound Leaf with Pinnate Veins

Coniferous: Trees that retain most of their needles during the dormant season.

Crown: The living branches and foliage of a tree.

Deciduous: A tree that shed all leaves annually.

Evergreen: A tree with needles or leaves that remain alive and on the tree through the winter and into the next growing season. (Note: some trees may be evergreen in one plant zone but deciduous in colder climates.)

Hardwood: A term describing broadleaf trees, usually deciduous, such as oaks, maples, hickories, ashes, cherry, poplar, elms, and more.

Heartwood: The inner core of a woody stem, composed of nonliving cells and sometimes differentiated from the sapwood by darker color.

Leaf Shape: Leaves are described as being linear (like a skinny feather), oval, oblong, ovate (like an arrowhead), elliptical, lance-shaped, triangular, heart-shaped, compound (many simple leaves arranged opposite one another on a stem), and lobed. The margin of a leaf is described as being entire (smooth), undulated (wavy), finely or coarsely serrated, or doubly toothed or bluntly toothed.

Lobes: Projections that shape a leaf.

Margin: The edge of a leaf.

Native: Inherent and original to a geographic area.

Opposite: Two or three leaves that are directly across from each other on the same twig.

Palmate: Blades or lobes or veins of the leaf arranged like fingers on the palm of a hand.

Pinnate: Blades or lobes or veins of the leaf arranged like vanes of a feather.

Pistil: The seed-bearing organ of the flower. The pistil consists of an ovary, stigma, and style when present.

Lobed Palmate Leaf with Palmate Veins

Root Collar: On a seedling, the transition between the stem and the root, usually recognizable by a slight swelling.

Sapling: A small tree, usually between 1 and 3 inches in diameter at chest height and 15 to 30 feet in height.

Smooth Simple Pinnate Leaf

Seedling: A tree usually less than an inch in diameter and no more than 3 feet in height that has grown from seed (in contrast to a sprout).

Specimen Tree: A tree placed so people can gain the greatest enjoyment for the color, texture, scent, or other pleasures it provides.

Spurs: Stubby, often sharp twigs that are often mistaken for thorns.

Stamen: The pollen-bearing organ of a flower.

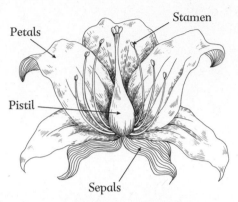

Flower Anatomy

Standard: This isn't exactly a botanical term in America, but
you will hear landscapers and horticultural workers sometimes refer to a "standard tree." They do this to differentiate
the height of trees in the same species. For example, a
standard Southern magnolia (*Magnolia grandiflora*) will
grow to height of over 80 feet. A dwarf Southern magnolia
like Little Gem (*M. grandiflora* 'Little Gem') will top out at
around 20 feet.

Teeth: Notches on the outer edge of a leaf.

Guidelines for Collecting Material

Viewing trees as simply a resource would be an easy approach to fall
into. I don't think we should do this. Trees are more than just grocery stores or hardware stores put here for us to take advantage of, in
my opinion. They are living and quite literally breathing entities that
should be treated with respect.

Obviously, anything that has been cast off by the tree is fair
game. Picking up leaves, nuts, or bark that has fallen around the tree

plainly doesn't harm the tree. The concern comes when you want to harvest from a living tree.

Make sure you have permission to gather the plants from the property. Just because the tree is growing in a vacant lot, that doesn't mean the property owner won't be concerned if you show up with a pair of loppers to cut material from his or her tree.

Trees are usually quite capable of taking care of themselves. They are accustomed to losing leaves and branches to animal, insect, and weather damage. They will, in most cases, heal over the damage and continue to exist. That doesn't mean that you might not cause harm when you clip off a significant number of branches or leaves. The rule of thumb is never take more than one-third of the available material. Make clean cuts with sharp tools to help the tree heal over the cut. Never cut a branch that is greater than three inches in diameter.

If possible, collect your material under the correct planetary sign for greater magickal effect. If you can't gather it in the correct sign, try to gather it in the correct phase of the moon. Material that is to be used for positive purposes is usually gathered in a waxing moon. Material to be used for baneful purposes such as breaking bad habits or warding is usually collected in a waning moon.

Finally, communicate your intent to the tree, especially if you are cutting something off the tree. It's the least you can do to show your respect for the tree and your environment. This doesn't mean you have to give long, flowery speeches to the plant. Simply explain what your need is and thank the plant for its contribution.

This is how we connect with our environment. I personally believe taking this step improves our magickal and ritual work. It demonstrates our understanding that we are a part of the greater community and that we respect the life energies within it.

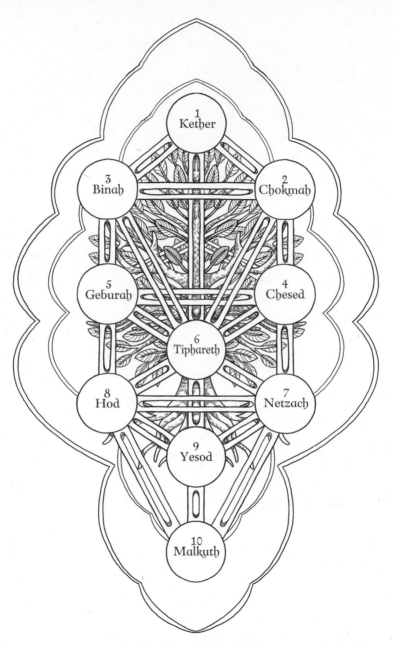

Kabbalistic Tree of Life

Conclusion

We've been around the world and through time looking for the Universe Tree. We've found a general reverence for trees. We've found trees as respected sources for wisdom, life everlasting, heroic inspiration, and more. We've found specific examples of trees as a model for the universe.

But what does it all mean?

That is a question that was posed to me one day while I was working at a local New Age outdoor festival. I was selling concrete yard art—small statues of Buddha and frogs, plaques of dragons and zodiac wheels, and other whimsical items with a Pagan theme.

A young man stopped to contemplate a plaque with a broad-canopied tree and equally broad root system enclosed in a circle—a common representation of the Universe or World Tree.

"What is this?" he asked.

I replied that it was a representation of the Universe Tree, what some people call the World Tree, to which he responded, "What does it mean?"

"That depends on your tradition," I explained. "Some see it as a metaphor for the interconnectedness of the world, with the top representing heaven; the middle, the mundane world; and the roots, the underworld or afterlife. Others see the tree as a kind of road map. It's a way to access other dimensions."

"How would that work?" he asked.

I tried to explain that some people meditate on the form, and depending on what their question is, they might use the canopy or the roots to journey in search of an entity to help.

He looked at me blankly and asked again, "What do you mean?"

I was momentarily distracted and looked away. When I turned back to answer him, he was gone. That left me with that broader question about the Universe Tree—what does it mean?

What are we supposed to do with this model of a broad-canopied tree with an exposed root structure? Can we press it into use in a modern world? Can we use it to help understand the world we live in?

Replanting the Universe Tree

It can be said without a doubt that modern history has provided society with countless examples of actions or deeds that defy logical or compassionate explanation. Despite the best efforts of what are considered traditional religions these days, countless bloody wars; senseless destruction of environments (natural and social) for profit or political motivation; cold, unthinking ennui in the face of suffering—these all seem to resist any rational explanations or solutions.

For better or worse, rationality is the currency of the realm in the modern world. It is the maze humans built for themselves when they fully embraced a scientific view of the world to the exclusion of all else. Gone are the pagan gods and pagan philosophy. Gone too is the watchmaker god of Christianity.

The concept of a watchmaker god was popularized in the late eighteenth and early nineteenth centuries as a way to reconcile the growing dominance of scientific thinking and methods with spirituality.[157] It was the uneasy compromise developed by rational thinkers of the day that allowed them to hold on to some semblance of deity in the face of all the contrary evidence in the lab.

The watchmaker was responsible for creating an exquisite natural technology—this world and all its interconnecting mechanisms of climate and animals and nature and science, everything that could be said to be involved in the smooth movement of the universe as a whole. In this model, God wasn't directly involved with the daily workings of the world. He didn't have to be. His "mechanism," his earth, would take care of itself just like a fine Swiss watch.

With no ever-present deity in the Age of Science and Industrialism, there was no "Other" who would demand sacrifice in exchange for taking responsibility for the world or shepherding the flock with a bottomless well of parental compassion.

Science and rationality became the new religion. It may have started in Western civilizations, but the concept has infected much of the rest of the world. Even when rationality fails to come up with a solution, society and its leaders seem to stubbornly turn back into the maze to look for another way out. What religion that is left has been reduced to "hearts and prayers."

Granted, science and rationality have served humankind pretty well. The pagan gods may have left, but so too did the monsters in the woods and caves that restricted movement and inspired fear. The watchmaker may have wandered off, but so too did the mindless demands for spiritually mandated bigotry and dominance over others

157. Adam R. Shapiro, "A Failed Concept for Intelligent Design," *Atlantic*, February 12, 2015, https://www.theatlantic.com/technology/archive/2015/02/god-watchmakers-and-the-short-half-lfe-of-technology-metaphors/385408/.

deemed less worthy, less holy—at least for the majority of modern readers as they review the past. Sadly, that hateful concept still endures for some in both the industrialized and non-industrialized world.

Still, we can't argue that science hasn't given the world better living conditions, better health outcomes, better ways to communicate among humans that can and have led to better relations (when the selfish and greedy don't intervene).

But science and rationality don't provide soul-satisfying answers to the question "What does it all mean?" It can explain the chemistry behind the tears shed at a funeral, but it can't explain the urge to believe in a hereafter where loved ones will be found again. It can explain the biology of the love that resulted in a wedding, but it can't explain the enduring feeling of devotion and compassion that makes couples stick together when their entire world is falling apart. Or the abiding sense of betrayal when no amount of trying can keep that world together.

The Universe Tree as Symbol

For that, humans need symbols and metaphors that allow them to be in contact with something more—something that is tangible but that doesn't require deep thought. Emotions are notoriously hard to render into words—the language of rationality and science. Deep, welling intense feelings don't translate sufficiently into words on a page, although in the hands of artists like Maya Angelou and T. S. Eliot, they come close.

We reach for this thing called spirituality when our rational mind tells us that a particular person is beyond redemption or that a situation is too flawed to fix. We still want to fix it, but we fail because we don't believe we have it within ourselves to generate enough energy to do the job. So we reach for a token or a symbol and pour our faith into it as though it were a great universal battery we can draw from that allows us to say, "I believe that I believe."

A proper example of this is in the 1939 film *The Wizard of Oz*. In this adaptation of L. Frank Baum's children's book, Dorothy, the Scarecrow, the Tin Man, and the Cowardly Lion face challenge after challenge and still end up on the Wizard's doorstep, begging for intelligence, a heart, and courage. They have all those qualities in great store. They simply don't believe they do. In the greatest of ironies, they are begging for those things from a charlatan, a con man.

So what does the Wizard do? He gives them tokens—symbols—in the form of a diploma, a heart-shaped clock, and a large medal. Only then do they believe.

Often we find when the conscious mind struggles to understand life and its complexities, it turns to the subconscious for solace. However, the language of the subconscious is symbols.

The Lovers card in the Rider-Waite tarot comes close to illustrating this conundrum. In it, the human on the right (logic) looks to the human on the left (emotion) as if for guidance. The human on the left looks to the spirit (inspiration) hovering above to receive that guidance. Upon receipt, that inspiration must be somehow translated back to language.

This is the paradox of the conscious and the subconscious mind. Humans can't speak directly to the Divine because language is a human construct and therefore limited. The Divine speaks to humans in signs and symbols, and it is up to the human to ferret out what the signs and symbols mean.

Fortunately, some symbols are easier to understand than others. According to Mircea Eliade, "It is through symbols that man finds his way out of his particular situation and 'opens' himself to the general and the universal. Symbols awaken individual experience and transmute it into a spiritual act, into metaphysical comprehension of the world. In the presence of any tree, symbol of the world tree and image of cosmic life, a man of the premodern societies can attain to the highest spirituality, for, by understanding the symbol, he succeeds in living the universal."[158]

The same is true for modern humans. In the symbol of the Universe Tree, we recognize that there is structure in the universe. That can be reassuring when the world around us appears to be falling apart. Far from succumbing to worries that "The end is nigh!" the Universe Tree reminds us that the world has been, is, and will always be—at least for the next five billion years when the sun is expected to burn out.

This leads to another truth, another meaning of the Universe Tree—that of resilience in the face of uncertainty and doubt. Author Hermann Hesse once wrote, "When we are stricken and cannot bear our lives any longer, then a tree has something to say to us: Be still! Be still! Look at me! Life is not easy, life is not difficult. Those are childish thoughts."[159]

When the summer rains blow through and disrupt our picnic, the tree under which we laid out our feast is not perturbed. When we learn of social unrest somewhere across the globe, the leaves on the trees in our yard fall, not out of sympathy, but because it is time in the natural order of things to fall. When we celebrate the arrival of a new child, the tree outside the hospital will still wait to bloom in a few weeks—not a minute sooner.

---

158. Mircea Eliade, *The Sacred and the Profane*, trans. Willard R. Trask (New York: Harcourt, 1987), 211.

159. Hermann Hesse, *Wandering: Notes and Sketches*, trans. James Wright (London: Pan Books, 1972), 52.

So much happens in our lives that seems earth shattering or paradigm shifting in the moment. Sometimes it is. Usually it isn't. The Universe Tree reminds us of this.

What was the most monumental thing that happened to you on the twenty-first day of class in the second grade? How certain were you that life would never be the same when you were jilted by your first love? When you set out on your first career path, were you absolutely certain that you would revolutionize your field? And did your life end when you didn't?

But we obsess on these points in time as if that slight in the second grade determined the outcome of our entire life or that we would never, ever, ever again find love or that we are total failures in the workaday world. It didn't, we did, and we're not.

Trees, in this case the Universe Tree, are there. The Universe Tree is always there. Despite winds and wars and romance and triumphs and missteps and fiascos—it is there. And so are we. We can endure. We always do until it is our time to return to the Divine, however we perceive the Divine. We endure as long as we don't let the winds, wars, romance, triumphs, missteps, and fiascos define our existence.

We too can send out deep, burrowing roots that tap the wisdom of past generations to lend us resilience in this generation. We too can stand strong in the present day, proud of our existence however that existence is manifest in the world. We too can reach to whatever we imagine the next existence to be beyond our canopy as something to be embraced and sincerely anticipated.

The Comfort of the Universe Tree

Not long ago, a young woman approached me at a New Age shop that I work at for a few hours a week. She had a few timid questions about candles and stones, explaining that she was "new to all this" and was still trying to find her way.

As she grew more comfortable in our conversation, she said she wanted to tell me something about a recent experience. While shopping in a thrift store, she happened on a brown stone into which someone had etched a large tree. The stone was strung on a chain as a necklace.

The young lady assured me she hadn't been looking for jewelry; she certainly hadn't been looking for a representation of a tree. She said she had seen similar trees on other pieces of art and clothing but had never been motivated to own them. However, this piece called to her, she said. It seemed as if she had rediscovered something that had been hers all along and she had simply misplaced it. Now it was back in her life, and she had to take it home with her.

The experience moved her, maybe even frightened her a bit. Now she had a need to know, what did it mean?

The obvious answer was that, in a subconscious way, the jewelry represented the rediscovery of a type of spirituality that she had always been drawn to and had only recently had the courage to explore. That was the rational, clinical explanation. And I told her that. I also explained, in brief, some of the ways people in the past revered trees, seeing them as models for the universe—a universal symbol of the universe that cultures across time and around the globe seemed to gravitate toward.

The young lady listened carefully, nodding her head. Still, as with the young man I spoke with many years ago, I felt she hadn't quite heard any more than a history lesson. She would have politely gone on her way, but I don't think she would have been totally satisfied.

Before I let her leave, I explained there was another way to view her prize. I would like to believe that I was struck by a moment of celestial inspiration. I was probably channeling some of the other more cultivated thinkers I had come across in all my reading for this book.

"Think of yourself as that tree," I said, signaling with my hand the area from my head through my midsection. "Your life in this moment is the trunk. You endure storms. You enjoy things that swirl around you. You grow and flourish in spite of or because of it all."

Reaching my arms upward over my head, I continued. "Up here, your mind and soul are reaching for the Divine, reaching for your spirituality. Your thoughts are reaching into the expanse and beyond the point that you can see."

Looking down, I said, "Your feet are rooted in the past. This part of you reaches down to your ancestral power, all those who have gone before, to help stabilize you and keep you strong and find the answers you seek."

The young lady looked at me and smiled. That was the answer she needed to hear on that particular day.

So we take this symbol of the Universe Tree as a token on a necklace or a fetish in our pocket or artwork on the wall and we meditate on it. We contemplate it. We empower that symbol with these realizations like we are charging a battery. Then, when we need that extra jolt to lift us up or power us on, we reach out and touch it.

It is an anchor in a turbulent world. It is a treasure box to hold our sense of security. We tether ourselves to it to weather the storms of our lives. In the good times, we bask under the comfort of its branches, knowing that we have a spot on this tree, in this place, at this time. And when it is time to move on, we have a road map that people in the past have traveled on before us.

It's all there in the roots and trunk and canopy of the Universe Tree.

Appendix of Trees

Here is a look at some of the trees you are likely to find in your own neighborhood, their descriptions, history, and uses for the magickal practitioner.

Apple

Latin Name: Malus

Range: Global

Parts Used: Flowers, leaves, fruit, bark, sap

Magickal Correspondences: Female, water

Uses: Love, beauty, longevity

Edibility: The fruits are edible. The remaining parts are unpalatable.

Warning: None known

Apples are native to China. The first species in this genus, *Malus sieversii*, is thought to potentially be 10,000 years old. Humans in Asia and Europe have been relying on the fruit for roughly 6,500 years, according to archeological evidence. Apples may have originated in Asia, but the plant spread eventually throughout the Northern

Hemisphere. There are 7,500 known varieties of apples in the world; 2,500 of them are in the United States.[160]

Description

A standard apple tree (*M. domestica*) will grow to about 25 feet in height. Dwarf trees reach 10 to 12 feet. Crab apple trees (*Malus* spp.) range in height from 10 to 25 feet tall.

The tree is deciduous with simple, slightly serrated leaves arranged alternately on the stem. Apples flower in early spring with a white to pink five-petaled flower followed by a single fruit. The bark of the tree is brown and scaly.

Expect standard apple trees to begin to produce fruit when they are 7 to 10 years old. Dwarf varieties and crab apples come into fruit a little sooner, roughly five years. The fruit ripens by late summer or early fall, depending on variety.

Expect to find mature apple and crab apple trees in many home landscapes, as the trees are often planted for their flowers more so than for the fruit, which can actually be a nuisance in late fall if it is not regularly gathered before rotting.

History and Lore

The apple tree is frequently sacred in most of the cultures where it is cultivated. Given the ease with which the plant cross-pollinates, it is little wonder that the apple is frequently the focus of many tales of love. It also has association with longevity and youth.

Deities associated with the apple include Venus (Roman), Aphrodite (Greek), Hera (Greek), and Idun (Nordic). Venus and Aphrodite are love goddesses. The apple tree has a special place among

---

160. "Apples Facts," University of Illinois Extension, accessed August 27, 2021, https://web.extension.illinois.edu/apples/facts.cfm.

the devotees of these goddesses. Pomona (Roman) is not a goddess specifically of apples but is often associated with them in her role as protectress of fruit orchards.

Hera is the Greek queen of the gods who owns the Garden of Hesperides, where a magickal apple tree grew with fruit that tasted of honey. The garden is a place near the ends of the earth, where everything is always in bloom and the trees never wither. The eleventh labor of Heracles was to bring some of those apples back to King Eurystheus. He had to outwit the giant Atlas and kill a huge, venomous serpent (possibly dragon) to gain the prize.[161]

The Greek goddess of strife, Eris, in a snit over not being invited to a party, created a golden apple and tossed it into the gathering with the words "for the fairest," etched on it. Hera, Aphrodite, and Athena vied to determine who should own it. Zeus was called to be the arbitrator but had more sense than to get into the middle of the argument. He tapped Paris, prince of Troy, to make the decision. After much behind-the-scenes bribery by the three goddesses, Paris chose Aphrodite as the winner. She fulfilled her promise to cause Helen, queen of Sparta and the most beautiful woman in the world at the time, to fall in love with him. Unfortunately, Helen was married at the time to Menelaus, the king of Sparta. When Paris spirited Helen away to his home, he kicked off the 10-year Trojan War.[162]

The Norse goddess of youth and spring is Idun. She tends a secret apple tree that produces fruit that when eaten confers youth, vigor, and immortality. These are given just to the Norse gods and

161. Morya Caldecott, *Myths of the Sacred Tree* (Rochester, VT: Destiny Books 1993), 95.
162. Edith Hamilton, *Mythology: Timeless Tales of Gods and Heroes* (New York: New American Library, 1940; repr. New York: Little, Brown & Company, 1969), 179.

goddesses to sustain their beauty and immortality.[163] In fact, the apples are called "the Age-Elixir of the Aesir."[164]

When Loki lured Idun away from her duties, she was kidnapped by a giant, and all the Norse deities aged quickly. Loki's deceit was discovered and he was forced to retrieve Idun at great risk to himself. The giant was vanquished, Idun returned with her apples, the Norse gods and goddesses feasted on them, and all was well again.

Uses

The fruit of apple trees is used in many traditions during harvest festivals to dress the fall altar. They can be used any time to honor deities involved with the harvest or specifically with apples.

Common European folklore advises those who wish to know the identity of their future love to carefully peel an apple and toss the long, unbroken string of peel over their shoulder. Use the shape of the peel to divine a letter or a name. This will be your future companion.

Whole apples can be peeled, decorated with clove buds, and dried to make talismans for winter solstice celebrations. This is often done with citrus fruit. In the case of apples, pick a firm type of apple, such as Crispin, Granny Smith, or Braeburn. Peel the apple, then use the clove buds to create a design. This can be as elaborate as you like, with a pentacle, runes, or special sigils, or you can just create simple bands of cloves running around the apple.

Spear the apple on a dowel or stick and set the stick in a pot of sand or florist foam to dry over a 2-to-3-week period. Make certain the spot you pick has good air circulation. Drying can be done in

---

163. Rosalind Kerven, *Viking Myths and Sagas* (New York: Chartwell Books, 2017), 65.
164. Snorri Sturluson, *Skaldskaparmal*, in *The Prose Edda*, trans. Arthur Gilchrist Brodeur (New York: American-Scandinavian Foundation, 1916; Sacred Texts, 2001), 131, https://www.sacred-texts.com/neu/pre/pre05.htm.

an oven at the lowest possible setting but the project will need to be monitored carefully.

The finished project can be decorated with seasonally appropriate ribbons and presented as talismans for abundance and love (apple) and protection (clove).

Asḫ

Latin Name: Fraxinus

Range: Temperate zones of Europe, Asia, and North America

Parts Used: Leaves, wood

Magickal Correspondences: Masculine, fire

Uses: Prosperity, health, strength

Edibility: Generally not used for food. The bark can be used as a mild laxative.

Warning: None known

Ash trees are linked most often in the minds of Americans of European descent with Yggdrasil, the Nordic World Tree. But they have a place in many other traditions.

Description

In the United States, we have a veritable crayon box of ashes with the white ash (*Fraxinus americana*), the green ash (*F. pennsylvanica*), the blue ash (*F. quadrangulata*), the red ash (*F. profunda*), and the black ash (*F. nigra*). There are also Carolina ashes (*F. caroliniana*) and Texas ashes (*F. texensis*). Most of these have limited regional ranges. The green ash is the one most commonly found from the Rocky Mountains eastward.

The height of the tree can range from 30 to 80 feet with a conical canopy. The leaves are simple and lance shaped. They appear opposite each other in a pinnate compound structure. The bark of the tree is furrowed with scaly ridges.

The tree has an inconspicuous flower in spring followed by a cluster of seedpods or "keys." The keys are aerodynamic with a long, tan, narrow wing that causes the seed to whirl on the breezes of autumn.

History and Lore

The ash tree belongs not just to great Norse mythology but also to the Greeks. In Hesiod's poem *Works and Days*, Zeus created the third race of men from ash trees.[165] They weren't as good as the races made from gold (the first creation) or silver (the second creation). However, Hesiod said they were strong and aggressive—perhaps too aggressive, as they ranged about making war with their weapons of bronze. Eventually, the ash-men killed themselves off entirely and Zeus had to start over again.

Among the Norse, the chief god Odin famously hung himself on the world ash tree, Yggdrasil, for nine days in order to learn the secrets of the runes. He and his brothers created the first human man from an ash log.

Among the Irish and British, the ash was treasured for its ability to protect.[166] Its wood was used for spears, bows, and chariot axles. The wood also came in handy for furniture and tool handles as it still does today. Three of the magick trees that protect Ireland are

---

165. Hugh G. Evelyn-White, trans., *Hesiod, Homeric Hymns, Epic Cycle, Homerica*, Loeb Classical Library Volume 57 (London: William Heinemann, 1914), 13.
166. "Ash Mythology and Folklore," Trees for Life, accessed August 30, 2021, https://treesforlife.org.uk/into-the-forest/trees-plants-animals/trees/ash/ash-mythology-and-folklore/.

said to be ash. The other two are the oak and yew.[167] Ash are also said to be favored by fairies, along with the oak and the hawthorn.

Uses

In magick, ash leaves are said to be healing. Many books on folk magick suggest placing ash leaves in a bowl of water by the bed to prevent illness. This must be replaced every day to be effective.

According to J. H. Philpot, the tree has associations with love. Philpot was a nineteenth-century author who produced a number of books on the place of trees in religious traditions. In her book *The Sacred Tree*, Philpot quotes folklore that says when a person goes out with an ash leaf in their glove, the first person they meet will be their true love.[168]

Of course, the Yule log is the most common association with the ash tree. The tradition of burning the Yule log at the winter solstice may have started with the Norse, but it has been adopted throughout European and American communities.

The original custom was to burn an entire ash log over a 12-day period as the sun stood still in the sky (according to pagan traditions). It had to be lit with a piece of the Yule log from the previous year.[169]

Fireplaces big enough to accommodate an entire log are few and far between these days. In America, it has become commonplace to decorate a small 12-to-18-inch long piece of ash. One to three holes in which to insert red or white candles are drilled in the wood. The bases of the candles are decorated with evergreen material from

167. Jacqueline Memory Paterson, *Tree Wisdom: The Definitive Guidebook to the Myth, Folklore and Healing Power of Trees* (San Francisco: Thorsons, 1996), 153.

168. J. H. Philpot, *The Sacred Tree: or, The Tree in Religion and Myth* (London: MacMillan, 1897; Project Gutenberg, 2014), 253, https://www.gutenberg.org/files/47215/47215-h/47215-h.htm.

169. Mandy Barrow, "The Yule Log," Project Britain, accessed August 30, 2021, http://projectbritain.com/Xmas/yule.htm.

other traditional winter plants, such as ivy, holly, pine, or cedar. These are kept in the days leading up to the winter solstice. Then the wood is burned afterward in a ritual to mark the passing of the year and to invite prosperity and protection into the circle.

If even this is a bit more than can be done due to a lack of a proper fireplace or fire pit, try mincing up some ash twigs and mixing the material into a seasonal incense blend of frankincense and pine. This can have the same effect of calling in prosperity and protection for the coming year.

Aspen

Latin Name: Populus

Range: Cooler regions of North America, Europe, Asia

Parts Used: Leaves, wood

Magickal Correspondences: Masculine, air

Uses: Protection from theft and metaphysical danger, eloquence

Edibility: Limited. The roots, inner bark, and stem bark are used as an antiseptic and analgesic.

Warning: May irritate sensitive stomachs and those with ulcers.

Aspen has the reputation for being the most widely distributed tree in North America. But you might be forgiven for having never seen one up close. Aspens prefer the cooler temperatures of higher elevations and more northerly latitudes.

Description

Aspens (*Populus tremuloides, P. grandidentata*) have a narrow canopy supported to an average height of 30 to 70 feet. The leaves are long, rounded at the base and finely saw toothed. The shiny green leaves turn golden-yellow in autumn—a signature that lends to the appeal of this tree. Authors and poets love to rhapsodize about the glow of a forest of fall aspens.

The bark of the tree tends toward white until it reaches full maturity, at which time the bark will often age to a dark gray. The trunk is smooth during the tree's youth but more furrowed with age. The flowers are long brown catkins that turn into tiny seed caplets that are basically worthless. The aspen tends to propagate by root expansion.

History and Lore

Aspen trees were frequently cited in old English literature as boundary trees. In some circles at least in the 1500s, the tongues of gossipy women were likened to the leaves of the quaking aspen or "aspe" tree, in that their tongues "taketh little ease and little rest."[170]

The bark and leaves of the aspen are used in folk medicine as an aspirin substitute. This makes sense because aspen is a member of the Salicaceae, or willow, family. Willows are a well-known source of salicylic acid.

Because the tree's wood dries to a very tight and light weight, aspen wood was often used for oars.

Among the Greeks, aspens are associated with the underworld. Heracles was said to have brought an aspen branch back from the banks of the river Acheron, one of five rivers that run through Hades.[171] He had journeyed there to fight for Alcestis, the wife of his friend, King Admetus. Alcestis had sacrificed herself so that her

---

170. Henry N. Ellacombe, *The Plant-Lore & Garden-Craft of Shakespeare* (London: Edward Arnold, 1896; repr., Mineola, NY: Dover Publications, 2017), 20.
171. Pausanias, *The Description of Greece*, vol. 2 (London: R. Faulder, 1794), 40.

husband could live. Heracles wrestled Thanatos for the right to bring her back to the land of the living.

Uses

Given its association with the underworld, aspen can be used to speak with the spirits from beyond the veil. Use the ground wood in an incense blend along with lavender and sandalwood to raise the vibration during séance sessions.

Another use relies on a unique characteristic of the aspen. While aspens can reproduce by seed, they also use suckers to spread into surrounding areas. They essentially "clone" themselves by sending up suckers along their root systems that then mature into full-grown trees. According to researchers with the US Forest Service, aspen clones can cover as much as 100 acres.[172]

The next time you host a community ritual, gather a handful of aspen twigs and wrap them securely with a long length of ivy (*Hedera*). Establish your sacred space according to your tradition. After honoring your deities and local spirits, pass the aspen and ivy bundle around the circle. Ask each participant to send their energy into the bundle, visualizing their spiritual roots going out to the other participants, uniting them in this special time and place. After everyone has blessed the bundle, add it to the fire pit. If you don't have or can't use a fire, place the bundle on the altar and continue whatever workings you have planned for the gathering. At the end of the ritual, have the leader of the group or a trusted member take the bundle to a wooded area and respectfully bury it to send your intentions out into the universe.

---

172. "How Aspens Grow," US Forest Service, accessed August 29, 2021, https://www.fs.fed.us/wildflowers/beauty/aspen/grow.shtml.

Bay Laurel

Latin Name: *Laurus nobilis*

Range: Warmer regions of North America, Europe,
  Mediterranean

Parts Used: Leaves

Magickal Correspondences: Masculine, fire

Uses: Psychic powers, wishes, protection, strength

Edibility: The leaves are used in cooking. They can also be
  used in teas, in limited amounts.

Warning: Overindulgence can cause vomiting and diarrhea.
  Eating large numbers of whole leaves can cause bowel
  obstruction because the leaves are not digestible.

The bay laurel was a much-prized plant around the Mediterranean
Sea, where it became ubiquitous to the culture after spreading from
its native South Asia. In addition to being a feature at the Oracle
of Delphi, boughs of the plant were used to honor athletes in most
sports and conquering heroes, home from the battlefield. Because it is
native to a subtropic zone, most people will not be able to grow a bay
laurel outdoors. However, the plant works very well in pot culture.

Description

Bay laurel gives us the cooking herb used in roast and stew recipes.
It is not the skip laurels (*Prunus laurocerasus* 'Schipkaensis') or Otto
Luyken cherry laurels (*Prunus laurocerasus* 'Otto Luyken') found in
most modern Western landscapes. These landscape plants are shrub
form, topping out around 10 feet tall with an 8-to-12-foot spread.
They grow in zones 6 to 9.

Bay laurels can reach up to 20 feet or taller in their native Mediterranean habitat. The leaves of all laurels are oval. Bay laurel leaves

are rather thin and leathery. The green of the leaf is dull and lighter underneath. This contrasts with our landscape laurels, which have thicker leaves with a richer green color.

The leaves of landscape laurels and bay laurels do share one common trait. Both have significant side effects when consumed in large amounts. All parts of landscape laurels are downright toxic—causing dilated pupils, panting, and, in extreme cases, shock.

Bay laurel oil is said to produce a sense of drowsiness or mild trance. This doesn't come through when bay is used a few leaves at a time in cooking. However, the Pythia, or high priestess, of Delphi was said to chew many bay leaves before giving answers to the questions of supplicants. Others believe the Pythia was said to have become intoxicated by some form of fumes issuing up through a fissure from the chasm below her tripod seat. And we shouldn't discount the belief of the devout that the Pythia was supposed to be in communication with Apollo himself during her trance state.

Because they require warm temperatures of zone 8 and higher, most American gardeners relegate their bay laurels to a container that can be moved inside and out with the seasons. This keeps Daphne as a bit of a pygmy.

History and Lore

Daphne, or more precisely, Dafni, is the name the Greeks gave the plant. Daphne was a dedicant to Artemis, a nymph who loved the hunt and not much else. According to legend, after a disagreement with Eros, Apollo succumbed to his nephew's arrow and pursued Daphne.[173] She had also been struck by Eros's arrow, but this one caused her to reject Apollo's advances above and beyond her pledge to remain an

---

173. Thomas Bulfinch, *Bulfinch's Mythology* (New York: Grosset & Dunlap, 1913; Project Gutenberg, 2018), 20.

unspoiled virgin of the hunt. Eros is known, as all lovers can attest, to have a wicked sense of irony.

When she found she could not outrun Apollo's advances, Daphne prayed for help. In some myths, Gaia either transforms the nymph into a laurel tree or whisks Daphne to Crete and leaves a laurel tree in her place.[174] In others, Daphne prays to her father Peneus, a river god, for help. He turned her into a laurel tree. So she ended up safe from Apollo's grasp but hardly free to enjoy the rest of her existence. Such is life for humans and lesser deities in Greek mythology.

Uses

Both bay laurels and landscape laurels have rather limited uses. Landscape laurels are pretty to look at and very practical in the landscape, but the wood has little or no commercial use.

Bay laurel gives us many culinary, cosmetic, and traditional medicinal uses. A few leaves in a soup or stew enriches the flavor of the pot. Bay oil is a germicide and insecticide. A strong tea made of 3 to 5 leaves is said to help with sore throat or stomach upset. A leaf or two stewed in a pot of beans is thought to reduce the chance of embarrassing flatulence.

Around the world wherever bay laurel has been grown, it has been seen as a source of wisdom and psychic ability. The oracles at Delphi may have chewed the leaves, but you don't have to go that far to reap the spiritual benefits. Burn bay leaves in the coals of your ritual fire and inhale the fumes as you meditate on the answers you seek.

It is also a source of protection. The Roman emperor Tiberius is said to have always carried a bay leaf with him to protect himself from thunderstorms and magickal attacks. A tea of bay leaves can be brewed

---

174. "Daphne," Theoi Project, accessed January 13, 2021, https://www.theoi.com /Nymphe/NympheDaphne.html.

and then sprayed around the entrances to the home for protection. Or do as the Chinese are said to have done. Use bay leaves in the mop water to cleanse and protect the home. By the same token, you can add bay leaf tea to a bath to cleanse yourself from negative influences.

If you would like to have your own source of wisdom, you can grow bay laurel in a sunny window. All you need is a loose, sandy potting mixture, a regular water routine to keep Daphne in the moist well-drained environment she likes, and a lot of patience. Bay laurels aren't rampant growers. But slow and steady is a good trait for a houseplant. If you have the opportunity to take your bay laurel outdoors during warm weather, keep it in a partially shaded location. The plant doesn't like strong sunlight, despite what you might imagine the Mediterranean climate to be like.

When well cared for, bay trees are said to live for decades in the container. This makes the plant a living heirloom that you can pass on to a fortunate sibling or friend when it comes time for you to move on in your journey.

Beech

Latin Name: Fagus

Range: Northern and Central Europe, North America

Parts Used: Leaves, nuts, bark, wood

Magickal Correspondences: Mixed

Uses: Wishes, to make wands

Edibility: All parts are edible, nutritious even.

Warning: None known

Mother Beech is the queen of the forest, known for her resilience and her height that can challenge the tallest oak. Our ancestors valued beech leaves for stuffing mattresses in the days before box springs and cotton batting. The leaves and the bark yield a usable dye for fabrics. No wonder people felt fortunate to have beech trees on their property!

Description

Beech (*Fagus grandifolia*) is a gray lady in the forest on the eastern seaboard of the US with smooth, mottled gray bark that unfortunately encourages some to etch their names on the surface, including, according to American legend, Daniel Boone. He allegedly carved "D. Boon CillED A. BAr on tree in the YEAR 1760," on a tree near Johnson City, Tennessee, many years ago. Maybe he did or maybe he didn't. However, the legend did inspire many a copycat.

The tree will generally heal, which leaves a legacy for the property owner, young lovers, or vandals for years to come. Ancient Saxons and Germanic tribes tended to remove the bark before writing on it.

Europe has its own beech, *F. sylvatica*, or copper beech. This one has been planted in the United States, but the native tree is by far the most commonly seen beech stateside. Both trees get very large, 60 to 80 feet, with tall, loose canopies.

The leaves are soft green, roughly serrated, and oval with a long tip. They are one of the last canopies to break out in the spring and one of the last to leave us in the fall. Many a time I have stood mesmerized in a snowstorm or light sleet storm, listening to the frozen flakes brush through the tan leaves or *pling-pling-pling* through the dead canopy.

Most people don't notice the tiny male flowers, focusing, if they do so at all, on the female catkins. These mature into beechnuts that split in the fall, providing a feast for local wildlife and people too.

History and Lore

Beech tree wood can be worked for furniture. When it's used as firewood, I can attest it makes a raging, hot fire. Archaeological studies indicate many European tribes used it to make charcoal.

When papermaking was limited, people turned to other natural sources to make records. Beech was one that was selected. The Old English word for beech is *bōc*.[175] When druidry was commonplace in Britain (roughly the fifth century BCE to the third century CE), the tree was considered a storehouse of knowledge. Eating the beechnuts was a way that one might access that knowledge. People of the period were known to make written records on thin slices of beech wood. This may be why some scholars believe that *bōc* could be the origin of our modern-day word for "book."

Europeans use the wood to smoke food. Drying hops on the beechwood racks is said to produce a smokey flavor German beermakers are wont to favor. Not surprisingly, an American beer company with German roots, Anheuser-Busch, still uses beechwood spirals through which it matures its beer in a process called beechwood aging.[176]

Uses

Beechnuts mature in September and October depending on the region, making them perfect additions to Samhain and Yule feasts. The nuts should be gathered and cleaned from their spiny hulls and thin triangular shell. The nuts can be dried in a warm, dark place for about two weeks. Once dry, the white nuts can be roasted in a

---

175. *Merriam-Webster*, s.v. "beech (*n.*)," accessed June 3, 2022, https://www.merriam
-webster.com/dictionary/beech.

176. Bryan Derr, "Brewmaster Blog: Beechwood Aging," Anheuser-Busch, July 23, 2013, https://www.anheuser-busch.com/newsroom/2013/07/brewmaster
-blog-beechwood-aging.html.

pan until lightly browned. The resulting product can be mixed into cookies or bread dough.

Gathering beechnuts is a labor-intensive project that requires a serious commitment. Another way to utilize the magick of beech in a ritual is to gather the leaves, green or dry. Set up your ritual space according to your tradition. After honoring your deities and local spirits, mark the leaves with your wish. Since beech leaves are only about three inches long, it is best to use symbols, runes, or sigils to indicate your desire. Once the ritual is done, take your leaves to the forest and cast them on the wind. If you can do so from a high spot, so much the better. Your wishes can also be tossed into the running water or a stream or river. Just let nature carry your wishes into the universe.

Birch

Latin Name: Betula

Range: Throughout the Northern Hemisphere

Parts Used: Bark, stems, wood

Magickal Correspondences: Feminine, water

Uses: Purification, to make besoms, protection

Edibility: The bark, leaves, and sap are considered safe and
   tasty food sources.

Warning: None known

When I earned my money doing landscaping, it was a rare home-owner who didn't want a river birch (*Betula nigra*) somewhere in their landscape. It is a midsize tree with interesting exfoliating bark that makes a nice focal point wherever it is planted. Added benefits include being deer resistant, easy to grow, low maintenance, and an excellent choice for wet areas around the home.

What many of the homeowners really wanted was a white paper birch (*B. papyrifera*). Sadly, the paper birch is better adapted to colder climates north of zone 7 in the US.

Description

The most common birch in my area is the river birch. It is usually grown with a multistemmed trunk, much like Southerners like to grow their crepe myrtles. The feature that homeowners and commercial property owners enjoyed was the exfoliating cream and tan bark, especially in the winter when there is so little to admire in the landscape.

Those same homeowners and commercial property owners occasionally regretted their decision when the tree matured and the massive root system began to selfishly hog all of the water and nutrients in the surrounding soil. That same root system would also wreak havoc on patios and sidewalks, heaving pavers one way and another. The messy twig drop in fall and winter tended to be a turn-off as well.

The one-to-two-inch long, saw-toothed leaves, fortunately, were less of a problem. I also rarely heard anyone complain about the male flowers, female catkins, or the little cones that followed them.

While Southerners and those on the Atlantic seaboard enjoy the river birch, New Englanders get to feast their eyes on the classic white paper birch (*B. papyrifera*) and the silver birch (*B. alleghaniensis*) with its slightly fragrant foliage that smells a bit of wintergreen. The Northwest has the red birch (*B. occidentalis*), one of the family members that doesn't feature peeling bark.

Europeans have a white birch as well that is also called the weeping birch (*B. pendula*) for its pendulant branches. All these trees reach between 30 and 70 feet at maturity, depending on location and species.

History and Lore

Birch wood is fine grained and a favorite of crafters and furniture makers. It is especially prized by makers of musical instruments for its resonance qualities.

An oil properly infused from the leaves is said to make a good massage treatment for sore muscles.

According to Moyra Caldecott, the birch tree is the guardian of the door to the sky for Siberian shamans.[177]

In a legend from the Ojibwe of the northern Midwest, white birch trees get their black markings when a young boy named Waynaboozhoo is sent by his grandmother to get fire from Thunderbird, a powerful spirit.[178] The boy changes himself into a rabbit and heads into the forest. He eventually finds the home of Thunderbird and begs to be let inside briefly to warm himself. Thunderbird agrees. When Thunderbird isn't paying attention, Waynaboozhoo rolls in the fire, setting his fur alight. He races from Thunderbird's home with the spirit in mad pursuit, flinging lightning bolts at the thief. Waynaboozhoo calls out for someone to protect him. A white birch offers to hide him. Waynaboozhoo escapes unharmed, but the white birch is forever scarred with black marks from the ricocheting lightning bolts.

Uses

As indicated, birch grows in such a way as to make perfect besoms. "Besom" comes from the Old English word for broom, *besma*.[179]

---

177. Moyra Caldecott, *Myths of the Sacred Tree* (Rochester, VT: Destiny Boos, 1993), 5.

178. Conley Aurora, "How the Birch Tree Got Its Marks," University of Wisconsin Oshkosh, accessed August 20, 2021, http://www.uwosh.edu/coehs /cmagproject/ethnomath/legend/legend10.htm.

179. *Merriam-Webster*, s.v. "besom (*n.*)," accessed June 9, 2022, https://www .merriam-webster.com/dictionary/besom.

While people used to use besoms for everyday cleaning, modern Pagans use them ceremonially to cleanse a space of negativity. Fortunately, they are quite easy to make.

Find or cut a birch stick roughly four to six feet long and at least one inch in diameter. This will be your handle. To attach the birch twigs to the handle, use leather strapping or heavy garden twine.

The material you cut for the head of your besom should be 12 to 18 inches in length. Start by securely tying one of the stems to the bottom of the stick about six inches up from the base. Once it is firmly attached, add another stem to the left of the first and tightly wrap the twine around both stems. Continue adding stems, firmly wrapping each one as you go, until the tool is as full as you would like. I recommend tying one circle of stems to the bottom six inches of the handle. Then, move up another six inches and tie another circle of stems to the handle. This will make for a nice, full besom. Finish the tool by creating a collar on the upper six inches, wrapping the entire top of the stems with your leather strapping or twine to give the tool a finished look.

Magickal tools should be dedicated. Prepare your ritual space according to your tradition. Have your besom on the altar. After calling the appropriate deities or guardians, take it up and cleanse it in the smoke of a purifying incense such as frankincense, sage, or copal. Next, purify it with blessed water or water that has cleansing essential oils mixed in. Ask your patron deity or guardian to bless and empower your new tool as well.

Bodhi Tree

Latin Name: Ficus religiosa

Range: India, South Asia, Indochina

Parts Used: Entire tree

Magickal Correspondences: Masculine, air

Uses: Meditation, wisdom, peace

Edibility: The figs of the bodhi tree are edible but unpalatable. The leaves and bark can be used in medicine.

Warning: None known

The bodhi tree is known by many names, including peepal tree, sacred fig, pipal tree, bo tree, and, as mentioned earlier, Ashvattha tree. It is a giant, growing over 90 feet tall, and unless you live in a tropical area, chances are you won't be able to grow one of your own outdoors. Luckily, the bodhi tree is not averse to living indoors.

Description

The bodhi tree is found throughout the Indian subcontinent, well into Asia, Southeast Asia, and the islands that populate the southern seas. They have been imported to the New World as well, currently being found in Florida and South America. While the tree is held in such high regard in many religions, it is considered a weed in Hawai'i and some other areas due to the aggressive nature of certain trees in this plant family, which have root systems that can crack concrete and strangle other trees. *Ficus religiosa* is not thought to be so rude. Its roots aren't aggressive.

The evergreen leaves are heart-shaped with a long tip and prominent leaf veins. Statues of the Buddha are often seen with the deity seated, silhouetted by the bodhi leaf. The tree trunk has smooth gray bark, flecked with brown specks. It is often seen with buttressing roots. *F. religiosa* produces figs in summer that are generally not eaten by humans except in times of hardship. However, wildlife loves them.

History and Lore

The history of the bodhi tree as it relates to Buddhism has already been covered in the chapter on Universe Trees and doesn't need to be rehashed here.

As a few other notes, in Hinduism, the bodhi tree is thought to be the embodiment of Vishnu. Other legends say that Vishnu was born under the bodhi tree. Vishnu can be enticed to inhabit a particular bodhi tree in your landscape if the proper ceremony is performed. Once completed, the tree is then thought to be a source of blessings.

In another Hindu tradition, the wood of the Ashvattha tree and Sami tree (*Senegalia polyacantha*) was used to create a sacred fire to reunite two lovers, Pururavas and Ilā.

Uses

When not being used as a landscape specimen or a place of meditation, *F. religiosa* is considered a source of many traditional medical treatments. The leaves are astringent and antibacterial. A tea of the leaves can be used as a laxative, as can the fruit, assuming you can tolerate the taste. The bark yields a dye for cloth and fiber for paper.

But of course, its key purpose for the metaphysical student is as a focus for meditation. This can be a bit tricky. As noted earlier, the bodhi tree grows in tropical regions. Even for those folks who live in tropical climates, a lot of land is needed to accommodate a bodhi tree.

You might consider looking to one of the bodhi tree's cousins like the weeping fig (*F. benjamina*) or the rubber tree plant (*F. elastica*). Both are common houseplants. While both can get very tall, growing in a container seems to slow them down a bit. The rubber tree is perhaps the easier of the two to grow. It needs bright, indirect light and regular watering during the growing season. Wipe its broad, glossy leaves off from time to time and you have a happy houseplant.

The weeping fig can be more temperamental. As a frequent fixture in bank lobbies and shopping mall common areas, you might think it is a tolerant sort. Like the rubber tree plant, it likes bright indirect light and regular watering. But move it and the tree will pout by dropping its leaves. Expose it to cold drafts and it will pout. Look at it harshly and it will pout. Well, that last bit may be an overstatement, but the point is a weeping fig needs the security of its own little spot in your home and the knowledge that you won't ask it to move.

F. religiosa does lend itself to bonsai. *Bonsai* is the Japanese term for growing really big trees in really small containers. The technique requires skill, artistry, and patience. The result is a living sculpture that will live for decades if well tended. The National Arboretum in Washington, DC, has a Yamaki pine bonsai that is over 392 years old. The Crespi Bonsai Museum in Italy houses the oldest known bonsai—a ficus that is believed to be over 1,000 years old.

Whether you purchase a bodhi bonsai, a rubber tree, or weeping fig, you can set up your own meditation area in a quiet corner of your home. Technically, this is not an altar, although you will need to set the bonsai on a table or bookshelf. Because you are tapping into another culture's tradition, it should be important to you to respect those traditions. You can include a water feature and a place to burn incense if you like. However, making a gaudy display with lots of trinkets, bells, and whistles goes against the grain. Remember, in Buddhist and Hindu traditions, the goal is to divest yourself of attachments to worldly possessions.

All you should need is a quiet place to meditate, a place to try to connect to the Divine. You don't have to assume a yoga position. Sit on a chair if that is more comfortable. This is a place where, for a brief period, you release your connections to the mundane world and focus on the journey of the spirit.

Elm

Latin Name: Ulmus

Range: Asia, South Asia, Europe, North America

Parts Used: Leaves, wood

Magickal Correspondences: Feminine, water

Uses: Elf magick, love

Edibility: The nuts and inner bark are edible. The inner bark of *U. rubra* is used to make a sore throat medicine.

Warning: None known

Once upon a time, there would have been no reason to describe the American elm tree (*Ulmus americana*). American streets were lined with them. Shipbuilders, furniture makers, and homebuilders relied on them. Then, a shipment of European elms was introduced to the country around 1930 and carried with it a plague called Dutch elm disease. The disease swept through the country, almost wiping out the American elm.

Fortunately, plant breeders have made major strides in hybridizing new varieties of elm that are more resilient against Dutch elm disease. The tree is hopefully on a comeback. In the meantime, we will have to make do with some of the lesser elms to take advantage of the magick of this tree.

Description

If you can find an American elm, it will be one of the taller trees in the vicinity. American elms can get to be over 100 feet tall. The winged elm (*U. alata*) is a bit shorter at 40 to 80 feet. The Chinese elm (*U. parvifolia*), imported to address the demand for elms in light of the decline of the native species, averages around 50 feet in height, while the English elm (*U. procera*) gets closer to its American cousin at 80 feet. Slippery elm (*U. rubra*), predominant in the Midwest to the East Coast, can reach heights of 70 feet.

All elms have elliptical leaves that vary in thickness and are arranged alternately on the stem. The tree trunks have furrowed bark that varies in color from light to dark brown. The seeds, which follow light green flowers in the spring, are also elliptical with a flat key. The canopy of the tree is open and rounded or vase like.

History and Lore

The beauty and longevity of the elm tree gave it a special place in the hearts of American developers and homeowners. There is a reason why many East Coast towns have an Elm Street within their boundaries. Before the elm tree population was devastated by Dutch elm disease, the wood was used for everything from barrel making to paper production to hockey sticks.

In Norse traditions, the first woman is created by Odin and his brothers from a log. She is called Embla, which is thought to mean "elm." Her husband, Ask, was created from an ash log.

In Greek mythology, when Orpheus journeyed to the underworld to retrieve his wife, Eurydice, he stopped along the way to sing a love song to lull the inhabitants there. Where he stopped, a grove of elm trees sprang up.

Given its association with the underworld, it might be easy to jump to the conclusion that this is why elm wood was used for coffins. In fact, Maud Grieve records that, once properly dried, elm wood is very resilient against warping and cracking, and this is why it was preferred by undertakers of old.[180] It was not only used for coffins but also for ships' keels and bilge planks—even water pipes before the extensive use of iron. The inner bark was used to make ropes and mats.

Uses

Not all magickal correspondences come from the distant past. In the modern history of the United States, we have an important correspondence for elm in the Survivor Tree at the site of the Oklahoma City bombing of 1995.[181] On April 19 of that year, a domestic terrorist bombed the Alfred P. Murray Federal Building. Official reports indicate 168 people died and over 600 were injured. The site has since been turned into a memorial to the victims.

The elm tree in the park across the street from the bombing was a popular site for downtown visitors and building employees to sit and relax. Despite the power of the bomb blast, the elm held its ground, becoming a symbol of resilience in the face of tragedy.

Today the Oklahoma City National Memorial Museum sells elm seedlings to support its mission. If you have the space available, planting one on your property would be a way not only to honor the victims and survivors of that terrible event but to also bring a symbol of resilience and strength into your own life. Seedlings from the Oklahoma tree are *U. americana* and in theory may be susceptible to Dutch elm disease. However, the fact that the tree survived

---

180. Maud Grieve, *A Modern Herbal*, vol. 1, A–H (New York: Dover Publications, 1971), 282.
181. "The Survivor Tree," Oklahoma City National Memorial Museum, accessed August 31, 2021, https://memorialmuseum.com/experience/the-survivor-tree/.

not just the bombing but also the ravages of the disease may indicate it has a greater resistance to the blight. Such trees have been found in remote areas of the US. If this is a concern, however, blight-resistant elm tree species have been developed by the nursery industry and are readily available. Planting one would be a good way to invite strength and determination into your life.

Fir

Latin Name: Abies

Range: Asia, Europe, North and Central America, North Africa

Parts Used: All parts

Magickal Correspondences: Feminine, earth

Uses: Purification, to remove hexes

Edibility: All parts are edible

Warning: None known

Fir trees are the type of tree most people think about when they think of Yule or winter solstice trees. Like many, this category has many imposters. For example, the Douglas fir is not in the *Abies* genus—it is *Pseudotsuga menziesii*. Growing up in Piedmont North Carolina, my family called the Virginia red cedar a fir tree. It's not a fir and it's not a cedar either! It's a juniper (*Juniperus virginiana*). This is one of those times when it is important to check your nomenclature before you harvest your plant material.

Description

Firs are evergreen. They will tend to lose the oldest needles toward the interior of the tree around May or June, depending on where they are planted. This seems to cause homeowners no small amount of alarm. But as long as the yellowing is confined to the interior of the tree, there is usually no problem.

Common fir trees in the United States include the balsam fir (*A. balsamea*) and Fraser (*A. fraseri*). Frasers are limited in their natural habitat to the Blue Ridge Mountains in North Carolina, southwest Virginia, and eastern Tennessee, preferring to grow in areas above 4,000 feet. Balsam firs are more common in the northern tier states around the Great Lakes and Canada. However, people are fond of trying to get both of these to grow at lower altitudes, and sometimes they succeed.

Fir needles are short, stiff, and deep green. They run around the branch, attaching to it as individuals, unlike pine needles that grow in a bunch of three to five needles. While in their natural habitat these trees can get as tall as 40 to 60 feet, in most home landscapes and parks, they are smaller, around 20 to 30 feet.

A healthy tree will have a dense canopy that can make it hard to see the trunk. The bark is smooth and thin. It's not unusual to see little blisters of resin along it. Older trees display ridged bark. As the tree matures, it will grow tight cones that are held upright on the branches. These are rarely allowed to remain on trees that are commercially grown for the seasonal market in December.

This genus has a number of other firs that grow naturally in the West and Northwest regions. However, they tend not to be as readily available to landscape or commercial markets.

History and Lore

In America, the fir tree is most often used as an ornamental and for holiday celebrations. Because the wood is brittle, it was never considered an important resource for anything other than making paper or plywood. The resin was valued for limited medicinal use either as a cold remedy or in ointments for wounds.

In a pinch, Native American tribes were said to use the inner bark for food. As with many evergreens in the Pinaceae family, burning the foliage was thought to protect tribe members from evil.

For both Pagans and Christians, the tree carries with it the symbolism of hope and everlasting life. In the depth of winter, many societies dressed their homes in evergreen boughs of all sorts to remind themselves that the dark and cold don't last forever.

Uses

Given the broad use of fir trees for holiday decorations, you don't have to worry about not living in close proximity to a natural stand of balsam or Fraser firs. After the holiday celebrations, you can dry needles from the tree you used in your decorations for future use.

Of course, you could just sweep up the needles that naturally fall from the tree in your home during the month of December. That's a bit messy and tends to include things like pet hair, dust, and who knows what else.

A better approach is to wait until it is time to take the tree down. After the ornaments are gone, cut as many branches from the tree as you think you would like to harvest needles from. The remainder of the tree should be chipped for mulch; used as a stand for things like fruits, seeds, and nuts to feed local wildlife; or tossed into a legally accessible body of water to provide a nursery for young fish.

Hang the branches you have collected in a dark, warm spot where they won't be disturbed. You can dry the branches in a sunny location, but this will bleach the color from the needles. Depending on the environmental humidity, it can take up to three weeks for the material to dry. When the needles break easily, the drying is done. You can also clip the needles from the branch and dry them in a food dehydrator.

Once the material is dried, it can be stored for up to a year in a sealed container. When ready to use, simply blend it with other herbs to create your own unique incense. Blend it with equal amounts of frankincense or sandalwood to create a purifying incense. Mix it with juniper and rosemary to make a healing incense. For use in breaking bad luck or hexes, blend your fir needles with dragon's blood resin and clove.

Hawthorn

Latin Name: Crataegus

Range: Asia, Europe, North and Central America, North Africa

Parts Used: Flowers, foliage, wood

Magickal Correspondences: Masculine, fire

Uses: Fairy magick, Beltane celebrations, protection

Edibility: Fruits and leaves

Warning: Hawthorn is used in traditional medicine for heart conditions and may cause low blood pressure or cardiac arrhythmia in some people. It may interfere with conventional medicines used for heart health.

Hawthorns may have the most magickal associations of any tree. From Greek deities of love and marriage to witches and fairies of all sorts, the hawthorn seems to have been beloved (or sometimes feared) by all.

Description

There are hundreds of hawthorns to be found in the forests of the United States. Some are regional, like the Reverchon hawthorn (*Crataegus reverchonii*), found primarily in southern Missouri, southeast Kansas, and parts of Texas. Others, like the green hawthorn (*C. viridis*), range from Delaware south to Florida and west to Texas.

All hawthorns are small trees rarely growing over 30 feet tall. The canopies are loose and open. A common feature on all hawthorns is a spine that can vary in length from one to two inches. This sharp thorn is actually a pointed branch and not a real thorn in the manner of a blackberry or rose thorn.

The leaves are elliptical, saw-toothed, and usually tinged with red when they first appear in spring. They grow in spirals around the branches. The flowers, which arrive in May or June depending on the region, are five-petaled, white, and held in clusters. As the season progresses, the tree makes red to orange pomes that look like berries. This isn't surprising since the hawthorn is in the same family as apples and pears.

History and Lore

Modern society is most familiar with hawthorn as an alternative supplement for heart disease. Like any herbal medicine, use of this herb is best coordinated with a trained professional. It doesn't work for all heart conditions and doesn't work for all people. No one should ever stop following standard medical practices for the management of heart disease without consulting a medical professional.

The wood of the hawthorn tree has never been important in either the furniture or building industries. It can be used for small tool handles but isn't considered appropriate for anything else.

In Europe, the trees are planted for hedgerows and field breaks, where they also provide food and shelter for local wildlife.

British magickal history is alive with uses for hawthorn, especially when it comes to fairies. When grown together with oak and ash trees, the threesome becomes a natural gathering space for fairies, it is said.

When young men went out in medieval England to go "a-Maying," they were looking for hawthorn trees from which to gather blossoms.[182] This was a celebration of the return of life after the dark, cold winter and had obvious fertility overtones.

The Glastonbury thorn is a hawthorn (*C. monogyna*) that is said to have been planted by Joseph of Arimathea one Christmas Eve many years ago, according to J. H. Philpot in her book *The Sacred Tree*.[183] He stuck his hawthorn staff into the ground that evening and by the next day, it had rooted and begun to leaf out. Sadly, the tree that was revered as Joseph's legacy was cut down in the seventeenth century under Puritanical influences. It has been replaced many times over the centuries with cuttings from other Glastonbury thorn offspring.

Oddly, this magickal tree also has associations with death. In Britain, it was believed to be very unlucky and dangerous to bring the flowers inside. To do so invited illness and possibly death into the household.[184]

The reason may be that the flowers are said to smell like death. I've never noticed any strong smell of any sort with the blossoms that I have cut over the years, but then, I'm probably cutting from a different variety of hawthorn than Englanders would be. Researchers have discovered that a chemical called trimethylamine is found in hawthorn blossoms—the same chemical that can be found in the decaying bodies of dead animals.

---

182. J. H. Philpot, *The Sacred Tree: or, The Tree in Religion and Myth* (London: MacMillan, 1897; Project Gutenberg, 2014), 144, https://www.gutenberg.org/files/47215/47215-h/47215-h.htm.

183. J. H. Philpot, *The Sacred Tree: or, The Tree in Religion and Myth* (London: MacMillan, 1897; Project Gutenberg, 2014), 164, https://www.gutenberg.org/files/47215/47215-h/47215-h.htm.

184. "Hawthorn," Trees for Life, accessed September 30, 2021, https://treesforlife.org.uk/into-the-forest/trees-plants-animals/trees/hawthorn/.

Whether the flowers actually smell of decaying flesh or the spirit of death lingers around them, it might be best not to take any chances. Enjoy your hawthorn blossoms outside.

Uses

Given its associations with fairies, you can honor these entities in your landscape by planting a hawthorn from a well-stocked nursery like Snowbird hawthorn (*Crataegus ×mordenensis* 'Snowbird') or Toba (*Crataegus ×mordenensis* 'Toba'). Or you can go a-Maying around Beltane yourself in your surrounding landscape. If you live near a forest or natural area, you should be able to locate a specimen somewhere among the forest population.

Hawthorns bloom from April to early June depending on the region. The wood is fairly nondescript if you don't know what you are looking for. However, the canopy should be in leaf by May, and you should be able to see the simple, elliptical leaves with that signature red tinge on the margins. After asking permission, gather some of the boughs in flower for your Beltane celebration.

Use them to dress the altar or to make garlands for the hair of your lady-love or young dandy. After the celebration, respectfully carry the branches and flowers to the edge of the woods as an offering to the Fae folk in your neighborhood. While you are at it, leave behind a little honey and milk so that the fairies can enjoy the festivities of Beltane too.

Hazel

Latin Name: Corylus

Range: Asia, Europe, North America

Parts Used: Nuts, wood

Magickal Correspondences: Masculine, air

Uses: Protection, fertility, luck, wisdom

Edibility: Nuts

Warning: No known warnings for this tree.

Hazel trees come with their own alias—in this case, filbert. Actually, the name *filbert* is most often applied to the large *Corylus maxima*. Whatever we call them, the nuts from this tree are a chocolatier's delight. Frankly, many desserts benefit from the addition of hazelnuts. Add to this the fact that the hazelnut tree grows quickly to a manageable size and produces nuts sooner than most other nut trees, and you have reasons beyond its significance in mythology to source a tree for yourself.

Description

Hazelnut trees can be considered large shrubs or small trees, depending on the species and the way they are pruned. The plant grows to a height of between 8 and 20 feet with about a 15-foot spread, often with a multistemmed trunk. The leaves are roundish to heart-shaped with a serrated edge and are a bit fuzzy.

The flowers come on in late winter as both female and male. As frequently happens in nature, the female flowers aren't particularly showy. However, the male catkins droop in a delightful fashion, like two-to-three-inch long creamy white tassels. Given that so little is going on in the landscape at this time, this an endearing quality to homeowners. American hazelnuts (*C. americana*) self-pollinate;

European hazelnuts (*C. avellana*) do not. You'll need two or more European hazelnut trees if you hope to harvest a crop from this species.

An intriguing specimen for the landscape is the Harry Lauder's walking stick (*C. avellana* 'Contorta').[185] The first plant was found in a hedgerow in England in the mid-1800s. The plant is sterile. It does not produce nuts. It does grow in a fascinating habit, branches twisting and turning without encouragement from the gardener. The plant is said to have been named for a famous Scottish entertainer, Sir Harry Lauder, who was rarely seen without his signature twisted and gnarly walking cane.

History and Lore

The history of Ireland and England is fully tied up in the hazelnut tree. At the head of the River Boyne the Great White Goddess Boinn dwelled, her home surrounded by nine sacred hazelnut trees. The river itself was a source of wisdom but so too were the hazelnuts.

Fairies were said to favor hazelnut wood. For this reason, hazelnut wood was generally avoided for firewood. Witches were said to use the wood for wands and for dowsing. Dowsing is the practice of finding water by using a forked branch from a special tree. We are most often told that willow wood is used, but in ancient Ireland, a forked hazelnut branch might have been preferred.

In the Fenian Cycle of Irish legends, those who wished to join Finn McCool's band of warriors had to pass a number of grueling tests, including fending off attacks from McCool's warriors with only

185. Kim E. Tripp, "*Corylus avellana* 'Contorta,'" North Carolina State University, accessed March 31, 2022, https://jcra.ncsu.edu/horticulture/plant-profiles /details.php?ID=64.

a hazel stick and a shield. In fact, McCool's name translates to "son of the hazel."

In Scottish tradition, October 31 is Nutcrack Night. The divination worked in a couple of ways. A young lad or lass could scratch the names of potential sweethearts on hazelnut shells. The nuts were tossed into a fire. The first to crack was the one destined to be the seeker's true love. In another test, lovers could scratch their names, each on a hazelnut. These were placed in the fire. If they cracked and jumped apart, the relationship was doomed. If the nuts rested and roasted peacefully together, a successful partnership was foretold.

Legends about the hazelnut aren't limited to the British Isles. Hermes, the Greek messenger god, was believed to carry a hazelwood staff for the wisdom it bestowed. As Hermes was the god of travelers and merchants, the hazelwood staff also lent him protection on his journeys. The hazelnut tree was believed to be sacred to the Norse god Thor. If travelers found themselves caught in a thunderstorm, they might seek shelter under a hazelnut tree. It was thought the Norse god of thunder would protect them from lightning strikes.

Uses

The most common use for hazelnut trees is obviously the nuts. Given that plant hybridizers have worked to cultivate hazelnut trees with a variety of colorful foliage, the hazelnut has many benefits for landscapers.

Interestingly, the wood has been used in the past for a variety of purposes, including wattle fences, roof thatch, fishing poles, and basket weaving. The long whips or twigs produced by the tree lend themselves to another interesting use—that of coracle or currach boat construction. A coracle boat is essentially a large basket, woven in the same manner that an egg basket might be made. Over the basket is stretched an animal hide that was tarred. It wasn't really seaworthy, but it was an inexpensive, relatively easy-to-make water vessel for use by fishermen in Wales, Ireland, and Scotland on the many rivers and lakes of those countries.

The wood can be used for walking staffs and wands. If you have access to a hazelnut tree, try picking out a shoot and carefully bending a hook in the top while the shoot is still attached to the tree. Stake it in place and let it grow for a couple of seasons. This bend will harden to make a perfect shepherd's hook.

Hazelnuts ripen in late August. This makes them a great source for Mabon festivities and feasting. Try your hand at the divination described earlier. You don't have to limit yourself to questions of romance. Wondering which job choice is right for you? Take the nuts, scratch the job choices on the shells, and toss them into the fire. The first to pop and crack is the one this Tree of Wisdom is pointing you to.

For cakes and ale at the Mabon ritual, make your favorite yeast bread recipe. Once the dough has risen and is ready to shape, flatten it out in a layer roughly 12 inches by 14 inches. Sprinkle a half cup of brown sugar on the dough followed by a cup of crushed hazelnuts. Add a tablespoon of cinnamon and a half teaspoon of nutmeg. Dot the dough with butter.

Roll the dough up from the long edge. You can leave it in a loaf form or make it into a wreath shape. Let the dough rise again and bake according to the oven temperature and timing of your recipe. Once the loaf is baked, you can top it with any number of sweet treats, like a simple sugar glaze or shaved chocolate or a thinned apricot syrup. Or you can just have it plain as a perfect Mabon treat.

Hickory/Pecan

Latin Name: Carya

Range: Asia and South Asia, North and Central America

Parts Used: Nuts, wood

Magickal Correspondences: Masculine, air

Uses: Strength, abundance, prosperity

Edibility: The nuts and sap are edible.

Warning: None known

Perhaps it is best to start the discussion of *Carya* with a bit of clarification for both the layperson and the magickal practitioner. Hickory trees fall into two categories: true hickories and pecan hickories. The true hickory category includes shagbark, pignut, shellbark, and mockernut trees. The second category includes the pecan tree from which we get the nuts to make tasty pecan pies, plus bitternut, nutmeg hickory, and water hickory.

When you are gathering material for magickal workings, any tree in this category will do. However if you are a homeowner with a hankering for a pecan tree, be sure to check the Latin name on the tree tag. Otherwise, instead of getting home with a pecan tree (*C. illinoinensis*), you might just end up with a pignut (*C. glabra*) or shagbark tree (*C. ovata*).

Not surprisingly, there aren't any available legends about hickory or pecan trees from European folklore. Of the 18 known species, 15 are native to the United States and the other 3 hail from Asia. Scientists believe *Carya* once had a greater range but died back during the Pleistocene ice age roughly 2 million years ago. The limited range hasn't stopped the tree from becoming a valuable source of timber for furniture and more in the age of humans.

Description

Hickory trees are giants of the forest, growing to 60 to 80 feet in height. Their bark is usually grayish-brown, rough, and loose, giving them evocative names like shagbark (*C. ovata*), one of the more common hickories in the United States. The canopy is relatively dense, making this a nice shade tree if you don't mind the squirrels pitching nut hulls on you while you try to enjoy a late summer afternoon on the deck.

Some hickories are limited in range, like the one that produces pecan nuts. This tree prefers to grow in Texas, Louisiana, and southern parts of Alabama and Georgia. Others, like the pignut (*C. glabra*), cover the eastern United States from the Mississippi River to the Atlantic Ocean.

The leaves are long, narrow, and yellowish-green. They grow in leaflets oppositely on the tree stem. The leaflets are serrated and always grow in odd numbers on the pinnate compound leaf.

Most of the nuts are round and covered with a thick green hull. They are hard to crack except for pecans. Regardless of the thickness of the hull, wildlife loves them.

History and Lore

European settlers and explorers learned about *Carya* from Native Americans who considered it a vital food source, shares research horticulturist LJ Grauke at Texas A&M. William Bartram, an eighteenth-century American botanist, reported members of the Creek tribe in the area of South Georgia harvested bushels of hickory nuts. These were cracked and boiled. The oil, called hickory milk, was drawn off. Bartram said it was as sweet as cream. The nut meats were dried for use in cooking as well. The same Texas A&M research reports members of the Powhatan tribe had a legend in which a goddess gave the spirits of the dead a drink on their journey to the rising sun. It consisted of hominy corn and a liquid made from pounded hickory nuts and water called "pokahichary."[186]

Like the Native Americans, Europeans found plenty of uses for the wood as well. It was valued for making hoops for barrel caskets, gun stocks, tool handles, and various dyes.

Uses

Staffs are symbols of power and authority, regardless of the religious tradition or society. If you have a patron deity, you can often find a suitable wood to honor them and make a staff from that material. However, hickory is readily available wood in most places and provides a sturdy hardwood that will make a durable staff.

After you source your wood, it's time to work. I prefer to work on staffs in a waxing moon. If possible, if I plan to dedicate it to a specific deity, I work the material on that deity's special day.

I use an old sturdy pocketknife to remove any rough bark, the inner bark, and the dried cambium layer underneath. The wood is then dried or cured, usually for several weeks.

Next, it's time to sand the material smooth. The sanding can be done by hand or by electric sander. Sanding paper is divided into grades or grit. The lower the number, the coarser the grit. An aged hickory staff might require an 80 grit to start with in order to remove any leftover cambium layer of material. The goal is to get the staff to a smooth finish, almost satin like. You can tell from the feel when you've reached that point.

When the sanding is done, it's time for embellishment, if you want that. This could involve etching or burning symbols into the

186. LJ Grauke, "Hickories History," Texas A&M University, accessed August 25, 2021, https://aggie-horticulture.tamu.edu/carya/species /histsp.htm.

wood or attaching stones and crystals. It's up to you. The staff can be treated with any of several oils to preserve it. I have used linseed, tung, and teak oils on various projects to great effect. Plan on applying at least three coats, always sanding in between coats.

With the work done, a dedication of the tool is a good idea. This should be done during a waxing moon on the day special to your patron deity. If you don't plan to dedicate the tool to a particular deity, pick either Sunday (for masculine woods) or Monday (for feminine woods).

Set your sacred space up according to your tradition. Use a red candle. If you are dedicating the staff to a particular deity, use an incense that is pleasing to that entity. Otherwise, frankincense or sandalwood incense is appropriate. When you are ready, pick up your staff. Communicate in words or thought your need to the staff. Pass it through the incense and over the candle fire. If you are calling a deity, ask that deity to lend his or her energy to your working.

When you feel the energy in the staff, your work is done. Ground yourself and open your ritual space.

Holly

Latin Name: Ilex

Range: Global

Parts Used: Leaves, wood

Magickal Correspondences: Masculine, fire

Uses: Protection, good luck

Edibility: Only the leaves of specific hollies can be used in teas.

Warning: Most species of this tree are toxic to humans and animals. Birds, however, are not affected by the toxins in holly berries.

Hollies are ubiquitous in the landscape. They are hardy, have few pests, and come in all shapes and sizes. Although hollies without points on their leaves exist, the first image of a holly that comes to mind for most of us is probably a spiny-leafed one with bright red berries. The spines are what give hollies their reputation for protection. Some can be wickedly beautiful or beautifully wicked, depending on whether or not you have to prune them. The Chinese horned hollies (*Ilex cornuta*) that have naturalized in the woods around my house come to mind as a good example of this.

Description

Hollies are so commonly seen in landscapes and commercial plantings that they hardly need describing. While there are a number of species in this genus of about 480 types that are groundcovers and shrubs, *Ilex* also has its share of trees. North and South America have an abundance of holly species; Europe has one—*I. aquifolium*. The canopy of holly trees is typically full and pyramid or conical in shape.

These can be evergreen or deciduous, although the evergreen types are more prominent. Common evergreen species in the landscape include Nellie R. Stevens (*I. cornuta* ×*I. aquifolium*), Foster (*Ilex* ×*attenuata*), and American holly (*I. opaca*). Deciduous hollies include possumhaw (*I. decidua*) and winterberry (*I. verticillata*). Tree-form hollies can easily grow over 30 feet tall, but they are usually kept lower in the home landscape. Deciduous hollies tend to walk that line between being a very small tree or a very large shrub.

The leaves of the evergreen hollies are shiny, ranging from yellow-green to almost black-green, depending on species. Deciduous holly leaves have less of a shine. All holly leaves are simple, growing alternately on the stem. Some have one or more spines; others are spineless.

The flowers are very small and usually go unnoticed unless the bees swarm them in late spring. The flowers are followed by berries (technically, this is a drupe) that can be black, yellow, or varying shades of red.

History and Lore

Hollies are another evergreen with deep associations with winter solstice celebrations. Bringing ivy and holly into the home in December represented a balance of masculine and feminine energies as well as the hope for continued life after the bitter cold.

Both holly shrubs and trees were used as hedge breaks. Maud Grieve records in her herb volumes that when planted near a home or farm, holly was believed to repel poison and protect from the occupants from witches.[187]

According to a work by Richard Folkard, holly leaves can be used for divination. In his book, he writes the querant must pick nine smooth leaves from a she-holly on a Friday evening. While this is being done, no word must be spoken. By the way, she-holly is the one that has berries—at least according to Appalachian folk tradition. "The leaves must be collected in a three-cornered handkerchief, and on being brought home, nine of them must be selected, tied with nine knots into the handkerchief, and placed beneath the pillow. Then, sleep being obtained, dreams worthy of all credit will attend this rite," Folkard explains in detail.[188]

For practical purposes, the wood of the holly tree is used for small tools and specialty work in cabinetry. Holly wood is very white and dense. It is sometimes stained black as a substitute for ebony.

---

187. Maud Grieve, *A Modern Herbal*, vol. 1, A–H (New York: Dover Publications, 1971), 405.
188. Richard Folkard, *Plant Lore, Legends and Lyrics* (London: R. Folkard and Sons, 1884), 377.

Uses

Holly branches can be hung in the home or above entrance doors for protection. Of course, hollies can be planted around the home's exterior (if that is an option for you) to the same effect.

You can also create a wash to use in the home or to spray on entranceways to keep evil away. Gather a potful of holly leaves during a waxing moon. Because holly is a fire herb, it would be best to gather on a day governed by Mars or when the moon is in Aries, Leo, or Sagittarius. Boil a pot of water, enough to cover the leaves you have picked. Pour this over the holly leaves. Add other protective herbs to the mix, such as fleabane, St. John's wort, and sandalwood, if desired, and let it set until the batch has cooled.

Strain the mixture. If you have made a large batch, measure the liquid and add at least one-fourth of the volume of either witch hazel or vodka. Otherwise, put some of the mix into a spray bottle and use it to spray around the doors and windows of your home. The liquid can also be poured into mop water to wash the floors.

Juniper

Latin Name: Juniperus

Range: Global

Parts Used: Foliage, wood

Magickal Correspondences: Masculine, fire

Uses: Purification, protection, health

Edibility: Edibility of the berries depends on the species.

Warning: Certain species, such as *J. sabina,* produce poisonous berries.

Junipers were once a mainstay of American landscapes due to their rugged, durable, forgiving nature. They tolerate blistering sun, dry soils (once established), and low soil nutrients. Aside from a tendency toward problems with spider mites, the only problem with this plant is aesthetics. You either like them or you don't.

Description

In the landscape, junipers, like hollies, range from ground covers to 60-foot trees. Keep this in mind as you gather material for spiritual purposes. If you don't have access to an eastern red cedar (*Juniperus virginiana*) for example, you can always substitute blue rug juniper (*J. horizontalis*) or any of the many other juniper groundcovers or shrubs in the landscape.

You can identify junipers most easily by their scaly foliage. The foliage is evergreen and grows four leaves to a row, opposite each other on the stem. The foliage will also tend to be prickly and aromatic, smelling like pines or cedar. The foliage is borne on trees that are very columnar or teardrop-shaped and full to the ground when young. As the tree grows, the canopy becomes broad, though still more oval than round. In spring, the tree makes dusty blue, berry-looking cones in sizes that vary with the species. These will ripen to a dark blue eventually if the local wildlife doesn't snap them up. The bark is reddish brown and shreds easily.

There are pockets of native juniper tree species around the continental US, such as the southern red cedar (*J. virginiana* var. *silicicola*) in Florida and Pinchot juniper (*J. pinchotii*) in Texas, but the most common tree-form juniper is the Virginia red cedar. Its natural habitat runs from out west in Texas and Oklahoma up to the Great Lakes and over to the Atlantic seaboard.

History and Lore

The uses for juniper revolve primarily around the cones it produces, often referred to as "berries" in common literature. The wood of juniper trees is resistant to rot, making it a favorite among farmers for fence posts. But beyond decorative use or tool handles, there is no major market for juniper wood.

The essential oil produced from juniper has plenty of uses, from household to cosmetic to medicinal. Juniper oil, along with pine oil, was a frequent additive to household cleaners. The aroma was and is considered purifying and uplifting. In cosmetics, it has been used in skin care products, again for its cleansing nature.

Medicinally, juniper has been advocated for everything from flatulence to heart health. Maud Grieve lists it as a diuretic useful for heart and kidney conditions, as does Phyllis Balch.[189] As with any herbal supplement for health concerns, these should always be used under the direction of a trained professional.

Of course, the most famous use of juniper berries is for gin. In her book *The Drunken Botanist*, Amy Stewart notes the Dutch were distilling gin in the mid-sixteenth century.[190] They called it *jenever*. The British developed a taste for the product after coming to the aid of the Dutch in their war against Spain, calling it "Dutch courage." Mark Forsyth suggests in *A Short History of Drunkenness* that the fashion for gin was encouraged by the British King William III, whose father was, after all, originally from the Netherlands. William had the idea to promote the production of gin to manage

---

189. Maude Grieve, *A Modern Herbal*, vol. 2, I–Z (New York: Dover, 1971), 452; Phyllis A. Balch, *Prescription for Nutritional Healing*, 5th ed. (New York: Penguin Group, 2010), 116.
190. Amy Stewart, *The Drunken Botanist: The Plants That Create the World's Great Drinks* (Chapel Hill, NC: Algonquin Books, 2013), 172.

the economic impact of grain harvest fluctuations, according to Forsyth.[191]

His tactic may have worked a little too well. For a time, the British were swimming in gin. The social impact on the lower, poorer classes was terrible. It took years to address the problem with laws and taxes until the craze for gin eased.

In modern history, gin's reputation has improved, although it ebbs and flows in popularity. Currently there is a fashion for gin flavored with exotic botanicals beyond juniper berries. England's Queen Elizabeth II had even gotten in on the market, selling Sandringham Gin in limited batches made from herbs and other botanicals grown in her own gardens.

Uses

It is an easy matter to make an essential oil from juniper berries to use for purification. Gather two cups of juniper berries from the Virginia red cedar or any of the *J. communis* plants in your landscape. Remember not to use the savin juniper (*J. sabina*) if by chance it is in your landscape.

In a crockpot or in a pot set over very low heat, combine the berries with enough oil to cover the berries to a depth of one inch. Let the combination steep for at least 24 hours. After steeping, put the oil and berries in a clean, sterile jar. Make sure the juniper material is covered, leaving no berries exposed. This will help prevent the growth of mold.

Set the jar in a warm, dark place for at least 30 days. Check the mixture at regular intervals to ensure there is no mold growth. From

---

191. Mark Forsyth, *A Short History of Drunkenness, How, Why, Where, and When Humankind Has Gotten Merry from the Stone Age to the Present* (New York: Three Rivers Press, 2017), 151.

time to time, give the jar a good shake. After 30 days, strain the oil away and use it as you would commercially made essential oil for anointing people during rituals or for dressing entranceways to the home. This oil is not recommended for internal use, although it can be applied externally.

You can do a cold processing of the oil by putting the berries directly into a sterile container and covering them with enough oil so that no berries are exposed. Store in a dark place, but remember to shake the container from time to time. This will take up to six months to get a sufficiently strong concoction to use. After it has set for a proper time, strain the oil and keep it in a clean, sterile container until needed.

Magnolia

Latin Name: Magnolia

Range: Asia; South Asia; North, Central, and South America

Parts Used: Flowers, leaves

Magickal Correspondences: Feminine, earth

Uses: Fidelity, companionship, and marriage

Edibility: The flower and leaf buds of some species are used in Asian cuisine.

Warning: None known

Magnolias are ubiquitous in the imagery of the South, especially the evergreen southern magnolia (*Magnolia grandiflora*). When they bloom in early summer, they are glorious, filling the air with a sweet fragrance. In the winter, expect to see many a homeowner and florist take advantage of the impact of those large, glossy leaves to amp up any holiday display.

Description

The huge southern magnolia dominates the landscape whether it grows naturally from seed or is planted there by a homeowner. This tree grows to between 60 and 80 feet tall with an expansive, full, rounded canopy that starts out life full to the ground. Plant hybridizers have come up with "dwarf" evergreen magnolias that not infrequently end up 30 feet tall.

Given a choice, the evergreen magnolia will stay full to the ground. It is the homeowner or a grounds maintenance crew who will often limb the tree up above head height. There was a fad for a time in the 1990s to espalier dwarf magnolias against a building. Espaliering is a pruning technique that keeps a plant flat against a wall or other structure. It is most often used on fruit trees, but with dedication and constant monitoring it can be done with other plants as well.

The leaves are thick, lance-shaped, and shiny dark green on top with feltlike hairs underneath. They don't break down very easily in the fall and winter months. The bark of the tree is smooth and gray but will become more furrowed with age.

Tree guides will tell you the range of this tree in the wild is southern Louisiana, Mississippi, Alabama, Georgia, and much of Florida. However, it grows perfectly fine north to Maryland, roughly in the zone 7 range on the USDA plant hardiness map.

For cooler climates, look for one of the deciduous magnolias. These have large, light green leaves, gray bark, and a variety of flowers that can be strap like (*M. stellata*) or tulip shaped (*Magnolia ×soulangeana*).

All magnolias produce felty cones that range in color from light brown to reddish hues. When the cones mature in the fall, they reveal pretty red seeds.

History and Lore

Evidence of the magnolia shows up in the fossil record from over 30 million years ago. Researchers speculate that it grew extensively in the Northern Hemisphere before the Ice Age wiped it out in Europe. The tree is currently considered native in Asia and America. It has since been reintroduced into Europe as an ornamental.

Despite my best efforts, I can find no legends about the magnolia tree. American folklorist Robert Folkard, writing in 1884, briefly mentions that a single blossom kept in a bedroom overnight was rumored to kill the sleeper therein. He claimed Native Americans would refuse to sleep under a magnolia tree while it was in bloom because the fragrance was so overwhelming.[192] My mother would have certainly sympathized. She loved the flower, but the fragrance made her sick to her stomach. Still, I can find no god or goddess, no spirit who was believed to be the source of its name or responsible for any of its attributes.

Ornamental uses are still the primary benefit of this tree. It has limited uses for furniture, pallets, and paneling but not much beyond that. It does have a use in the making of wooden venetian blind slats due to its anti-warping properties.

In Asia, deciduous magnolia is used in many medicinal preparations. The National Institute for Biotechnology Information reports that health care providers in China and Japan use the bark from *M. officinalis* for treatment of anxiety, asthma, depression, gastrointestinal disorders, headache, and more.[193] It is also used in those countries

---

192. Robert Folkard, *Plant Lore, Legends and Lyrics* (London: R. Folkard and Sons, 1884), 423.
193. Mélanie Poivre and Pierre Duez, "Biological Activity and Toxicity of the Chinese Herb *Magnolia officinalis* Rehder & E. Wilson (Houpo) and Its Consitutents," *Journal of Zhejiang University Science B* 18, no. 3 (2017): 194–214. doi:10.1631/jzus.B1600299.

in dietary supplements and cosmetic products. The medicinal use in the United States is not widespread. In cases where it is used, it should always be provided under the care of a trained professional.

In the United States, both evergreen and deciduous magnolias are overwhelmingly used for ornamental purposes in the landscape.

Uses

Deciduous magnolias can be considered harbingers of spring, flowering as they do in late winter to early spring. Gather the flower petals and use them to dress an altar to welcome back the spring deities of your tradition.

Southerners use evergreen magnolia foliage to decorate for the winter holidays. It is a comforting reminder that winter doesn't last forever. Pagans with access to the evergreen magnolia might like to dress their Beltane altar with the sweet, fragrant flowers from that tree.

In the language of flowers popular in Victorian times, the magnolia flower was considered a symbol of nobility, perseverance, and the love of nature. The Chinese are said to associate magnolia with prosperity, luck, and marital bliss. Scott Cunningham listed fidelity as one of the attributes for magnolia in his book *Cunningham's Encyclopedia of Magical Herbs*.[194]

With that association in mind, you can make a fidelity powder from the dried flower of either the deciduous or the evergreen magnolia. Gather a handful of the petals and dry them thoroughly in an oven set on the lowest setting or in a food dehydrator. This will take longer for the evergreen magnolia flower than for the deciduous magnolia flower petals. Monitor the material, especially in the oven, to ensure you don't over-dry it.

---

194. Scott Cunningham, *Cunningham's Encyclopedia of Magical Herbs* (St. Paul, MN: Llewellyn Publications, 1985), 165.

Once dry, use a food grinder to reduce the material to as fine a powder as possible. Blend it with other fidelity herbs like red clover and cardamom if you like. This mixture can be sprinkled in the shoes of your companion or whoever you want to remain faithful to you. It can also be used around the home or wherever that person may come in contact with the powder. To extend the mixture, you can follow a practice used in certain African and Caribbean diaspora traditions and blend it with an equal amount of white cornmeal.

One word on the use of this kind of compelling magick: You should never use magickal skills to force someone to come to you or stay with you against their will. That comes with karmic consequences that you probably don't want to pay. This powder should be used in those cases where you are in a consensual relationship and maybe you're a little worried about someone else putting pressure on your companion to stray.

Maple

Latin Name: Acer

Range: Asia, Europe, North America, North Africa

Parts Used: Flowers, wood

Magickal Correspondences: Masculine, air

Uses: Love

Edibility: The sap is generally the only part used for food from this tree.

Warning: None known

Maples are among the most popular of landscape trees. They may be native to the eastern half of the United States, but varieties of maples are grown just about everywhere.

Description

Maples are found throughout the United States, Europe, and East Asia. The bark grows in varying shades of gray and starts out smooth but furrows with age. *A. griseum* has exfoliating bark that makes it a good focal point in the landscape.

Every young school child knows how to draw a maple leaf. With the exception of the boxelder maple (*A. negundo*), maple leaves are pinnate or five-pointed, and the leaf margin is coarsely toothed. Box-elders have compound leaves. Pinnate maple leaves can be full or fine. For example, there are varieties of landscape maples, such as some of the Japanese maples (*A. palmatum*), that have such delicate foliage they have earned the name "lace leaf maple" (*A. palmatum* var. *dissectum*).

These leaves fill the broad, rounded canopy of the maple tree, making this an excellent shade tree.

Red maple (*A. rubrum*) has the greatest natural range, covering most of the eastern half of the US. It is only matched by the silver maple (*A. saccharinum*). By the way, don't let the Latin name of the silver maple fool you. It's not the sugar maple of New England and Canada. That would be *A. saccharum*. Regardless of natural range, the red maple is a favorite landscape tree nationwide because of its red fall foliage. Hybridizing has intensified that red color but even in nature you can expect to see red, orange, and yellow colors in autumn that still make a beautiful statement.

Something else that fascinates children in the schoolyard is the tree's distinctive seedpods, called samaras. All maples make winged seeds in pairs that usually hold on to the tree in clusters. As they fall, children delight in trying to catch them on their helicopter-like flight pattern.

History and Lore

Maples are another of those trees that are key to the timber industry for use in furniture and building projects. At one time, maple was the preferred choice in flooring material for bowling alleys. For furniture, sometimes a perfect slab of lumber isn't the most desired choice. When maple wood is damaged by beetles and bacteria, the resulting patterns are called "figured" wood. The distinctive patterns are like free-form artist renderings, making for truly unique tables and cabinets.

Maple wood is a favorite resource of musical instrument makers. It is often used for the backs and sides of violins and various parts of guitars. Fender, maker of iconic guitars for decades, prefers to use maple wood for the necks of the company's instruments.

In New England and Canada, the sugar maple (*A. saccharum*) is a mainstay of the regional economy for the sap that is converted to syrup. In early spring as the tree sap begins to rise, farmers put a single tap in the tree and hang a bucket from it to catch the liquid that oozes out. Trees must be about 40 years old before they can be tapped. The sap is carefully boiled to reduce the water content to a point when the sap becomes a viscous syrup. It can take up to 40 gallons of sap to make one gallon of syrup.

English settlers learned about syrup production from Native Americans. Several tribes across the northern-tier states had legends about why maple syrup was processed in the manner it was. According to the Chippewa and Ottawa tribal legends, maple syrup once flowed from trees without any need for processing. But one day, the god NenawBozhoo decided his people had gotten too lazy to hunt and forage for food because they had such a luxury. He cast a spell on the tree that increased the amount of water in the sap, forcing his people to work for the sugary treat.[195]

Uses

In European traditions, maple corresponds to love. This might be due to the warm, rosy color of the leaves in fall. Or it could have something to do with the blush of red flowers on the maple trees in late winter and early spring.

Either way, you can use these parts of the tree to make a heart poppet to bring a little love into your life or wish a little love into the lives of your friends. In either the spring or the fall, gather the plant material for drying. In spring the flowers will come and go rather quickly, so don't wait too long. Gathering the red leaves in fall is a little more leisurely of an activity. Dry the material in an oven on the lowest setting or a food dehydrator. Watch it closely. Maple flowers and leaves are thin and delicate. They will dry quickly. The flowers won't need any additional work after processing. The leaves will need to be broken down into small bits.

Make heart poppets out of scrap material if you want your poppets to last for a while. If you plan on burning the poppets in a ritual fire or burying them in the woods, the poppets should be made of paper or something that will be biodegradable or burnable.

Depending on the type of love you are after (or that you wish for your friends), add appropriately colored rose petals to your maple herb. For example, you would use white for platonic love, pink for friendship, and red for passionate love. You can add red pepper and cinnamon for a passionate mix. Add some vanilla and catnip for a more playful love.

---

195. "Legends and Lore," Michigan Maple Syrup Association, accessed June 8, 2022, https://www.michiganmaple.org/legend-and-lore.

Fill the poppets and seal the edges. If this is a ritual for yourself, set up your ritual space according to your tradition with the poppet(s) on the altar. If you are working in a group, have the poppets in a bowl until the appointed time in the ritual when you can pass them out to the participants.

This would be a good time to call on the deities in your tradition who are associated with love. Ask them to lend their energy to your poppet(s) as you focus on sending loving energy into them as well. When you can no longer hold the idea in your mind's eye, put the poppet back on the altar and complete your workings. At the end of the ritual, you can burn the poppet in the fire or in a small fireproof dish, if you are working inside. When burning isn't an option, plan to go out as soon as possible to bury the poppet in the woods to send your desires out into the universe.

Oak

Latin Name: **Quercus**

Range: Asia; Europe; North, Central, and South America; North Africa

Parts Used: Acorns, bark, galls, wood

Magickal Correspondences: Masculine, fire

Uses: Strength, endurance, virility, protection, prosperity

Edibility: The nuts are edible and the bark is used in some traditional medicines.

Warning: None known

Variety, thy name could be *Quercus*. Oaks come in all shapes and sizes all across the United States—throughout the Northern Hemisphere, in fact. In recent years, researchers have divided oaks into New World and Old World. Of the 500 known species of oaks around the world, 50 are native to the United States.

Description

Most oaks are deciduous, dropping their leaves eventually. We have to qualify the leaf drop of deciduous trees because oaks are marcescent. The leaves change color and technically die but cling to the stem until they are pushed off the following spring.

The canopy is broad and full, usually pyramidal in youth but becoming rounded and ranging in maturity. The leaf shape varies with the tree. Leaves can be smooth-edged and lance-shaped like the willow oak (*Q. phellos*), coarsely saw-toothed like the chestnut oak (*Q. montana*), round-lobed like the white oak (*Q. alba*), or pointed and bristle-lobed like the red oak (*Q. rubra*).

Depending on the species, the leaf could have as few as three lobes, as with the water oak (*Q. nigra*), or as many as nine, as the white oak does. Some leaves are shiny; others aren't. Some leaves are thick, while others are thin.

The acorns vary as well. The seed is held in a scaly cup that could be flat or rounded or could just about cover the entire seed, as with the sawtooth oak (*Q. acutissima*). Acorns are preceded by catkins, much to the chagrin of allergy sufferers and those who own vehicles when the pollen begins to settle.

The bottom line is when it comes to oaks, a good field guide is invaluable if you are looking for a specific species.

History and Lore

Practically every society that had access to oaks revered the tree. Generally, they associated their primary deity with it, especially the sky deities. Given the many uses for oak, is it any wonder?

Everything from houses to boats was built from oak over the centuries. The Notre Dame Cathedral in Paris was built from a forest of oaks. It suffered major damage from a fire in 2019. In 2021, another forest of ancient oaks was being cut to help restore the structure to the same condition that it was in prior to the fire.[196]

The USS *Constitution*, Old Ironsides, was a warship built in 1797 and is still viewable today. It earned its name from a battle during the War of 1812 with Britain. In a sea battle with the British ship *Guerriere*, cannonballs from the enemy ship seemed to bounce off the *Constitution*'s hull without causing damage. The British sailors were heard to exclaim, "Huzzah, her sides are made of iron!"[197] Of course, they weren't made of iron—they were made of Georgia oaks.

In addition to buildings and boats, oak is used for furniture of all descriptions. Wine and whiskey barrels are made from the material. Wine, rum, tequila, cognac, brandy, gin—it seems plenty of other alcoholic beverage makers require the unique characteristics of a well-used oak whiskey barrel to mature their own libations.

The astringent qualities of oak make it useful in alternative medicines for diarrhea and antiseptic washes. Tannins in oak make it important to tanners of animal hides. The acorns are valuable food resources for animals, but they have also been used by humans. Everywhere oaks grew, humans learned which ones were immediately edible and which ones had to be soaked to remove excess

196. Nora McGreevy, "Hundreds of Centuries-Old Trees Felled to Rebuild Notre-Dame's Iconic Spire," *Smithsonian Magazine*, April 12, 2021, www.smithsonianmag.com/smart-news/dozens-century-old-oak-trees-felled-rebuild-notre-dame-cathedrals-iconic-spire-180977481/.

197. Ellen Fried, "Old Ironsides: Warrior and Survivor," *Prologue* 37, no. 1 (Spring 2005), n.p., https://www.archives.gov/publications/prologue/2005/spring/ironsides.html.

tannins before the end result could be dried, ground up, and used in breads or as a thickener and extender for stews.

Uses

Oak foliage can be used throughout the year to honor male deities. Use it to dress the altar or specifically to surround the candles for male deities. In our own group, the males have, from time to time, used oak foliage as headdresses to honor the Divine Masculine.

In certain European and Wiccan traditions, the Oak King is half of the aspect of the Horned God and rules the year from Yule until the summer solstice. After that, the Holly King takes over.

One year, my own group built its Yule ritual around a mock battle between the Oak King and the Holly King. Members divided up to cheer for one or the other combatant, waving different colored bits of cloth to show their preference. After a merry chase around and around the balefire, the two male volunteers wearing chaplets of holly and oak faced off in a battle with swords. Of course, the Oak King felled the Holly King and the seasons were set aright for the coming year!

In autumn, the acorns can be gathered to dress the altar as well. They also make good talismans for wishing spells. Gather plenty of acorns in a bowl and set it on the altar. At the proper time during the ritual, the leader of the ritual can carry the bowl around the circle, letting each member draw one or two acorns. During a guided meditation, members are encouraged to silently focus on their desire for the coming months or year. After the meditation, everyone hangs on to their acorn until the ritual is completed.

The acorn is then taken into the landscape or a legally accessible forest, where it is buried. As the acorn sprouts the next season, the wish is believed to be granted.

Persimmon

Latin Name: *Diospyros*

Range: Asia, North America

Parts Used: Leaves, fruit, pits

Magickal Correspondences: Feminine, water

Uses: Luck

Edibility: The fruit and leaves are edible.

Warning: None known

Persimmon trees are related to the tropical ebony tree (*Diospyros ebenum*), that tree that produces the rich black heartwood so prized by furniture makers and craftsmen. Since most of us aren't likely to ever make it to Indonesia or Sri Lanka to harvest our own, how convenient is it that we can find a cousin growing in the continental United States?

Description

American persimmon trees (*D. virginiana*) are loose in habit and canopy. They can grow up to 60 feet tall but are more often found around 30 to 40 feet in the wild. In the United States, it is native from Connecticut to Kansas, south to Florida and Texas. The Asian persimmon (*D. kaki*) has been cultivated in Asia for over 2,000 years. It has gained favor with gardeners in the United States, who can't always find the native variety grown in their nearby woods.

The leaves are basic green, smooth-edged, and, like most fruit-producing trees, lance shaped. The bark is dark brown to black and deeply furrowed.

In the late spring, male and female flowers are produced on different trees. The male flowers are clustered in groups of white-green, small, bell-shaped flowers while the female flowers are more off-white, larger, and borne singly. The fruit matures in late fall to early winter.

The fruit of the American persimmon is small, around the size of a ping-pong ball, and slightly flat. Like the flower, it is held very close to the stem until it drops off. You don't want to eat it until it drops off. Persimmon fruit is filled with tannins that will pucker your mouth. The general guideline among Southerners is to wait until after the first hard frost to go looking for persimmons. Once the orange fruit ripens, the meat is sweet and tasty and barely there. Persimmon fruit is almost all seed.

That is another one of the reasons why growers are more interested in Asian persimmons. The fruit ripens in about the same timeline but is about the size of a tomato. Seeing them on a leaf-bare tree in the dead of winter is a bit odd. Asian persimmon also has large seeds but provides much more pulp.

History and Lore

In Asia, persimmon wood is used for paneling and furniture. The persimmon tree in America is used more for specialty products like pool cues and textile shuttles. At one time, it was favored for use in golf club heads, but the sport has moved on to more modern materials today.

The greatest emphasis on persimmons is as a food source. Native Americans were known to use the fruit fresh and dried. Any Southerner worth his or her salt knows that persimmon pudding comes to market at county fairs and festivals after October. A well-made persimmon pudding is thicker in consistency than regular pudding, closer to the texture of a brownie. With eggs, milk, and spices, it is a fall treat to rival anything made with pumpkin spice.

California has a number of farmers who are growing Asian persimmons for the general market. In Asia, persimmon production is a significant industry. There, the fruit is dried to make a snack or the pulp is used in desserts, salads, and baked goods.

Use

Southern folklore has it that the persimmon seed holds the secret to the severity of the upcoming winter. Find a ripened American persimmon and retrieve a seed. Very carefully cut the seed from side to side to reveal the embryo plant inside. If the embryo is shaped like a fork, the winter will be mostly mild. If it is shaped like a spoon, the winter will be mostly snowy. If it is shaped like a knife, the winter will be mostly icy and "bitingly cold."[198] In my experience, the reliability of these forecasts is about as good as the groundhog's forecast for spring. But it's a fun way to spend an autumn afternoon.

Because it is in the ebony family of woods, persimmon shares the association of that wood for protection and power. An ebony wand is said to be a powerful tool for the practitioner who knows how to use it.

While it is possible to carve your own wand, persimmon wood is very dense and can be hard to work unless you have special tools. A better approach is to check specialty stores and online sources for persimmon veneer. Veneer is a thin sheet of wood used on top of other, easier-to-work or less expensive woods.

At a craft store, look for a plain wooden box of a size you can use to hold your magickal tools or herbs or essential oils—literally anything you might like to store securely or respectfully. Measure the surface area of the box to determine how much veneer you might need.

Cut the veneer to fit the sides, top, and bottom of the box. Using a wood glue according to directions, carefully adhere the veneer to the surface of your box. Let it dry. After the glue dries, you can stain the box an appropriate shade for your purpose. The box can also be etched with a cutting tool or woodburning tool to feature symbols

---

198. "Persimmon Lady's 2019–20 Winter Forecast," Farmer's Almanac, last modified March 25, 2021, https://www.farmersalmanac.com/persimmon-seed -prediction-69619.

unique to your tradition. Seal the finished product with a clear or satin varnish to preserve your work.

As with any tool, the box should be ritually cleansed and purified before being put into use.

Pine

Latin Name: Pinus

Range: Northern Hemisphere and limited parts of the
  Southern Hemisphere

Parts Used: Cones, foliage, bark, wood

Magickal Correspondences: Masculine, air

Uses: Health, protection, purification, fertility, virility

Edibility: Pine nuts and needles are used.

Warning: None known

Like the oak tree, pines can be found all across the United States and the globe. Where they don't grow naturally, pines are frequently grown in landscapes as specimen trees or in forests for the valuable wood the trees produce.

Description

Pines are evergreen conifers that can be tiny, around 10 feet tall, or skyscraping at over 250 feet tall. Most will average between 30 and 70 feet tall. The bark is deeply fissured and scaly, even on the white pine (*Pinus strobus*) and cedar pine (*P. glabra*), which start life with a smooth bark. As with us humans, the furrows and ridges come with age.

The canopy of a pine generally begins full to the ground and pyramidal. Over time, most species limb themselves upward, producing a loose, towering top. A few like the Scots pine (*P. sylvestris*)

are maintained in a pyramidal shape to be sold as seasonal holiday trees in the winter. As an aside, this tree is often called Scotch pine in the US.

All pines produce needle clusters three to 15 inches in length, two to three to a bundle. Its bristly and scaly cones can be shaped like rounded ovals or long tapers. Some cones have sharp spines on the tips of the overlapping scales. The male cones produce yellow pollen that can rival oak pollen for its impact on allergy suffers. The goal of the male cone is to pollenate nearby female cones that will eventually dry into those lovely holiday decorating materials used in the winter. The end result in a particularly bad year (for humans) is thick clouds of yellow, sticky dust that settles on everything.

History and Lore

The history of the pine genus is the history of mankind. It has been used for food, cosmetics, medicine, and building material.

The inner bark is edible if not exactly savory. The needles can be brewed in hot water like a tea for a good source of vitamin C. Pine nuts are delicious whether in pesto or on salads.

While technically all pine trees produce seeds (referred to as nuts, although they are not true nuts), most will make rather small seeds. The pine nuts you find in gourmet and grocery stores usually come from Russia or China from *P. sibirica* and *P. koraiensis*.

Along with the tulip poplar, pine is an invaluable source of timber for building and for furniture making. While it takes the trees 20 to 40 years to reach maturity, pines are continually planted around the United States, just as some farmers plant corn or other food crops for harvest. The trees are also valued for pulpwood and resin products like turpentine.

The Clonycavan Man of Ireland is one of many bog people found over the years. He is estimated to have lived around the third or fourth century BCE. While debate swirls around how and why he died and ended up in a bog, there is no doubt about his cosmetic use. The man's hair was done up in a topknot and held in place with a gel mixture of oil and pine resin. We continue to use pine resin today in mascara, lipstick, and other cosmetics.

Uses

Pine cones are natural little carriers that make them perfect fire starters. We used to spend some evenings in the winter gathering buckets of white pine cones for Grandma to use in her wood stove. White pine cones are relatively tight in structure, but the cones of black pines, loblolly's yellow pines, scrub pines, and more have more open habits that just beg to be stuffed with something.

That something can always be lard. After filling the cone with lard, roll it in birdseed and hang the cone back outside to support your local wildlife.

For spiritual purposes, you can gather a number of cones and dress them to use in ritual fires. Dry the cones in the oven to get rid of any insects. This is one time when a food dehydrator won't work as well due to the size and shape of the cone.

Gather together wax and a variety of herbs. The herbs can be blended together to make appropriate mixtures for the various sabbats or for specific ritual workings, such as protection or prosperity.

Spread your herb mixture out on a cookie sheet or a sheet of foil. Carefully melt the wax. Using tongs, dip the cone into the hot wax, and then quickly roll the cone in the herb mixture. This can be done several times until you are satisfied that you have layered enough herbs on the cone.

Set the cones to harden on a second cookie sheet or sheet of foil. Once the cones have hardened, they can be individually wrapped in wax paper until ready for use or stored in a large sealable container.

Sweet Gum

Latin Name: Liquidambar

Range: Southeast and East Asia, North and Central America, the Mediterranean area

Parts Used: Sap, bark, seedpods

Magickal Correspondences: Masculine, air

Uses: Protection, exorcism

Edibility: The sap is edible.

Warning: No known warnings for this tree.

Sweet gum trees make great shade trees that also provide wonderful fall color in the landscape. People love the tree but hate the seedpods, so researchers developed a sterile, non-fruiting variety called *Liquidambar styraciflua* 'Rotundiloba'. It has all the attributes of the original without the burrs. But what witch would want to miss out on such an important resource as witches' burrs?

Description

The full Latin name for our American sweet gum is *Liquidambar styraciflua*. This tree can get 60 to 80 feet tall on average, but 100-foot tall specimens are not unusual. While it is a deciduous tree that loses its leaves in the fall, those leaves have a glossy look that might deceive you into thinking it is an evergreen. The leaves form almost perfect star shapes roughly the size of an adult's hand.

History and Lore

Sweet gum has a sturdy wood that makes it second only to oak in hardwood timber production. The wood is used for pulpwood, furniture, and plywood. Because it is related to the storax tree, sweet gum resin is used in perfumes and medicine.

Native Americans chewed the sweet resin as gum. A member of Hernando Cortés's band of conquistadors recorded in his journal that the Aztecs they met would also enjoy chewing sweet gum resin.[199] Beyond that, this is another American tree for which there is no recorded folklore.

Americans have a love/hate relationship with the sweet gum in the landscape. They love the shade from the tree canopy. They love the strong, straight structure of the tree. They love the beautiful red canopy in autumn. But they absolutely hate the rock-hard seedpods that fall in the later part of the year.

Sweet gum balls can't be crushed by lawn mowers of any size. They don't compost well at all. Stepping on them while barefoot is a pain. Stepping on them in shoes is an invitation to a sudden fall. All that can be done is to keep the pods raked up and hope for an early end to autumn.

Uses

I don't advocate tapping sweet gum trees for their sap. However, if you have to have a sweet gum tree cut down, it is worthwhile to see if you can collect the sap that will otherwise be wasted. Given the expense of European storax, it could be a nice investment of time.

Because they have a reputation for exorcism and banishing, just having sweet gum balls on the altar during a working can lend power to a ritual. Since sweet gum is in the storax family of trees, it also has protective energy. You can put this to good use as a talisman.

First, gather a bag of clean sweet gum balls. Dry them in an oven or food dehydrator to get rid of any insects. Next, you will need a

---

199. Rob Paratley, "Economic Botany & Cultural History: Sweetgum," Urban Forest Initiative, University of Kentucky, accessed September 1, 2021, https://ufi.ca.uky.edu/treetalk/ecobot-sweetgum.

glue gun. You will be creating a large ball of sweet gum balls. Start by gluing together three balls in a triangle. Next, glue a red ribbon that is about 24 inches long to the top of your triangle. You will use this to hang the talisman when you are done.

Then, add a sweet gum ball to the top and bottom of the triangle. Continue building the ball out until you have a ball that is aesthetically pleasing in shape and is as big as you like. You can embellish it with appropriate crystals if you like. However, remember that sweet gum balls carry a lot of protective power by themselves.

Do a ritual in which you charge and bless your talisman, preferably during a waxing moon. Then hang it in an entryway where it can do its work of protecting your home.

Tulip Poplar

Latin Name: Liriodendron

Range: North America

Parts Used: Wood

Magickal Correspondences: Feminine, earth

Uses: Passion, cleansing

Edibility: The bark and root are used in traditional medicines and for flavoring.

Warning: None known

Common nomenclature being what it is, the tulip poplar tree (*Liriodendron tulipifera*) is often confused with the aspen tree (*Populus tremuloides*). The two are quite different in range and appearance.

Description

The tulip poplar is found east of the Mississippi from Canada to Florida but has been carried west to California and east across the

Atlantic to Europe, where it is well received for its form and value in the timber industry. It grows naturally ramrod straight until it tops out at around 80 feet tall. The bark is grayish brown and smooth on young trees but well furrowed on mature trees.

The canopy is generally full, filled with shiny medium-green leaves that some might liken to maple leaves. They shouldn't. Maple leaves have five points; tulip poplar leaves have four tips. They can be quite large, as big as an adult's hand. The leaves turn buttery yellow in late summer and are among the first to fall with autumn.

In spring, the tree is filled with the flowers that give it its common name. They are cup-shaped with six greenish-yellow petals dabbed with orange at the base. The cup is filled with many thin pistils and thicker stamens. Birds and bees love them for the abundant nectar. As the flower fades, what is left looks like a cone but is actually a compact cluster of samaras that dry in autumn to release single-seed winglets.

History and Lore

This is another one of those trees for which there appears to be no folklore. Native Americans made good use of the tree, but they don't seem to have any stories about why it grows the way it does or why it has a tulip-shaped flower or why the leaf has its unique shape. Because the tulip poplar wasn't known in Europe or the Mediterranean countries, we have no myths to fall back on from these regions. When the Greeks or Romans talked about poplars, they generally meant the white poplar (*Populus alba*) or the black poplar (*P. nigra*).

Still, the furniture industry today would have a hard time existing without tulip poplar lumber. It is an inexpensive, fast-growing source of timber in a world that seems to always be hungry for building material. Given its naturally light color and its durability, the wood is a popular resource for furniture. The light coloring makes it easy to stain to mimic other, more expensive woods.

Because of its tight growth habit and light weight, Native Americans and early settlers would often carve canoes out of entire logs.

Most arborists love to herald the tree for its beauty and grandeur in the forest, and it is a spectacular tree. However, its very height makes it less than desirable as an urban landscape tree. For those with enough land to support its use, it is a beautiful addition to the property.

Uses

You can make use of the tulip poplar's little seedpods to create besom talismans for yourself and your friends. In autumn as the pods are dropping from the trees, gather them and carefully snip off the stem.

Dry the pods in a warm, dark space. Food dehydrators work well for this too. You can also dry them in the oven on the lowest setting. Just be sure to keep an eye on them so that they don't become too brittle. These pods will become the broom part of your talisman.

You need a boring tool and some thick skewers. Use the boring tool to carefully bore a hole in the stem end of the pod big enough to accommodate the skewer. You don't have to drill the hole out very deep. This may take a little practice until you develop the technique that allows you to make a hole without destroying the pod. Add a drop of glue to the hole and insert the skewer. The length of the skewer is up to you, but aesthetically, I would recommend a skewer that is twice as long as the pod. Leave the talisman to thoroughly dry.

Once the talisman is dry, decorate it with colorful yarn or thin ribbon to suit your purpose. The decoration can be blue for healing, purple for spiritual uses, or red for protection. Add a loop at the top, secured with glue, with which to hang the talisman.

Add a few drops of an appropriate essential oil to a tablespoon of alcohol or vodka. Use this to soak the besom part of the talisman. The essential oil should match your purpose, such as pine oil for health, frankincense for purification, or clove oil for protection. You don't have to leave the talisman soaking in the liquid. Just make certain to fully saturate it. Once it dries, it is ready to be placed in the work space, in the home, on the altar, or dangled from a car rearview mirror. Be sure to share some of your work with friends.

Walnut

Latin Name: Juglans

Range: Asia; southeast Europe; North, Central, and South America

Parts Used: Nuts, wood

Magickal Correspondences: Masculine, fire

Uses: Health, intelligence, wishes

Edibility: The nuts are edible. The leaves and bark can be used in traditional medicine; see warning below.

Warning: While the nuts are safe, modern medical sources express reservations about the safety of using other plant parts, citing the possibility of stomach upset and liver and kidney damage.

Besides oak and poplar, perhaps no wood is as often used in furniture making as walnut. It is a durable, rapidly growing tree with many uses.

Description

The deciduous tree itself can get quite large, easily growing to between 80 and 100 feet tall. Trunk diameters can reach over six feet wide. The bark of the tree is lightly furrowed and silver-gray in color.

Walnut leaves are composed of an odd number of smaller, oval-shaped leaflets that are bright green in color. Compound, alternate leaves are one to two feet in length. Each leaf has 15 to 23 dark green leaflets that are between two and five inches long and have a finely toothed margin. The leaves give off a pungent smell when crushed, not unlike hickory tree leaves.

Walnut trees produce male flowers on catkins and female flowers on terminal clusters where the fruit develops. Springtime allergy sufferers know when the tree is in bloom, as it causes them quite some problem for several weeks. You don't have to live near a walnut tree to suffer its effects. The wind will do an excellent job of carrying the pollen to your doorstep.

After the flowers come the walnuts—rock-hard green bombs that can dent a car or a head when they fall. As the nut matures, the skin turns black. The mush between the nut and the hull is treasured as a furniture, basket, and craft dye. It's even used to dye hair. Always wear gloves when handling mature walnuts, however. The dye is maliciously persistent.

History and Lore

When Europeans talk about walnuts, they mean *Juglans regia*. Americans would call this the English walnut while the English would call it the Persian walnut, given its origin in modern-day Iran.

This is the tree referred to in Greek legends as the origin of the Latin botanical name *Carya*. According to Robert Folkard, Carya was the youngest daughter of Dion, king of Laconia. Carya and her two sisters were blessed with the gift of prophecy by Apollo due to the respect Dion had shown for the god. When Dionysus or Bacchus came calling on the family, he fell in love with and slept with Carya. In a misuse of their gift, the other two sisters found out about it and tried to keep the lovers apart. Dionysius turned them into stone for their jealousy. Carya was turned into a walnut tree.[200]

In Roman traditions, the tree was considered unlucky, but oddly, the nuts were a favorite symbol of fertility. Later in history, medieval superstition held that the walnut tree was a favorite meeting place of witches.

Americans mean *J. nigra* when they talk about walnuts. The black walnut wood is resistant to decay and easy to work for furniture while being quite durable. Some sources tout the black walnut as a good shade tree. This doesn't take into account the fact that black walnuts exude a toxic compound called juglone that keeps most other plants from growing near it. This is a defensive mechanism called allelopathy. While the chemical is not toxic to humans, it can be residual in the soil for years. Walnut leaves and hulls that are composted tend to lose this toxicity after about six months.

Uses

You can use this special walnut trait in your protection spells for your home. Gather and dry the leaves from a black walnut tree. Once the leaves are dry, coarsely grind them into small bits. These can then be blended with other protective herbs, such as St. John's wort and garlic, and dragon's blood resin.

During a waning moon, preferably on a Tuesday or Saturday, set up your ritual space according to your tradition. Prepare yourself with meditation and by cleansing yourself with the smoke of frankincense or dragon's blood. Your herb mixture should be on the altar along with a red or black candle. When you are ready, take up the bowl or packet of herbs and focus on charging them with a

---

200. Richard Folkard, *Plant Lore, Legends, and Lyrics* (London: R. Folkard and Sons, 1884), 582.

protective, shielding energy. See the herbs sending out a radiating force field that keeps negativity and bad luck far from your home. Ask your patron deities and or ancestors to lend their energy to your work.

When you can't hold the image in your mind any longer, open the circle. Walk deosil around the house perimeter or property boundaries, sprinkling a little of the herbs as you go. Continue to see the shielding power of the herbs establishing a strong boundary between your dwelling and anything that might harm you and yours.

When you are done, re-enter the circle. Thank any helpers for their time and service. Ground yourself and complete your ritual work knowing you've taken an active step to protect what is yours.

Willow

Latin Name: Salix

Range: Northern Hemisphere, limited populations in the Southern Hemisphere

Parts Used: Leaves, stems, bark, wood

Magickal Correspondences: Feminine, water

Uses: Moon magick, healing, divination, love, exorcism

Edibility: All parts are edible.

Warning: None known

If some researchers are correct, the weeping willow (*Salix babylonica*) may be the tree referred to as the cosmic *halu-ub* or huluppa tree of Mesopotamian myth. Even without this cosmic image, the sight of the weeping willow is very evocative. It's a little sad but very peaceful as the graceful branches wave over a nearby pond or stream. It's hard to imagine that these trees were once considered a symbol of death and mourning. Such a pretty plant deserves much better than that.

Description

Willow trees can be found all over the country and around the world in moist growing areas. The majority are deciduous. A limited few in southern Europe are evergreen. The bark is brown to black and a bit ragged. The bark is a rich source of salicylic acid used in traditional medicine.

The leaves are typically elongated and lance-shaped with serrated edges. They are among the first to appear in spring, making them an early herald of the change in seasons. Most are yellowish green to dark green with a few sporting a bluish tint.

The tree produces male and female flowers in the form of catkins. If you have ever heard the term "pussy willow," it was likely a reference to the male flower that starts the season as a cute little kittenish, fuzzy bit of fluff. The female flowers aren't quite as cute, looking more like caterpillars.

History and Lore

Many goddesses are associated with the willow tree, including Artemis, Persephone, and Hera. In some Greek legends, Hera was said to have been born under a willow. The willow was sacred to Persephone as a tree of the underworld.

The pliable nature of willow branches made it a great resource over the centuries. Archeological record has been found of fishing nets made from it. Baskets, mats, furniture, fencing, and toys have been made of willow. In old Europe when daub and wattle houses were a regular feature of towns and farms, the wattle was not infrequently willow wood. The daub would have been the mud used to hold the structure together.

Jacqueline Paterson records many legends associated with the willow in her book *Tree Wisdom*. In it, she notes that the Sumerian god Bel and his consort, Belili, were deities of the willow tree. Paterson maintains that worship of Bel found its way to Britain through waves of migration over thousands of years. In time, the British came to worship Bel's day from the evening of present day April 30 to the morning of May 1, making this the start of Beltane.[201]

In keeping with the willow's association with death, Paterson said a Celtic custom held that planting a willow tree on the grave of the deceased would allow that person's spirit to enter the tree.

Among Chinese Buddhists, the willow is thought to chase away bad spirits. Given the ease with which willow can be rooted, the Chinese are also said to see the tree as a symbol of renewal and immortality.[202]

The willow's reputation in the field of medicine is extensive. It is a source of a natural anti-inflammatory that is helpful for everything from arthritis to headaches. Phyllis Balch's book *Prescription for Natural Healing* lists it as a possible source of relief for allergies, backaches, nerve pain, and menstrual cramps, among other disorders.[203] Balch also warns pregnant woman should not take the herb, nor should anyone who is allergic to aspirin. As always, get the advice of a trained professional before using any herb for health care.

Uses

Given the willow's association with Bel and Beltane, you can use pliable, fresh willow twig cuttings to mark the holiday.

---

201. Jacqueline Memory Paterson, *Tree Wisdom: The Definitive Guidebook to the Myth, Folklore, and Healing Power of Trees* (San Francisco: Thorsons, 1996), 257.

202. "Willow Mythology and Folklore," Trees for Life, accessed August 28, 2021, https://treesforlife.org.uk/into-the-forest/trees-plants-animals/trees /willow/willow-mythology-and-folklore/.

203. Phyllis A. Balch, *Prescription for Nutritional Healing*, 5th ed. (New York: Penguin Group, 2010), 128.

Before the Beltane ritual, gather enough soft wood twigs 30 to 36 inches long to make headbands for all participants. Braid three twigs together for each person in a long rope. Use this to make a chaplet to fit each person's head. The headband can be held in a circle with colorful ribbon or yarn.

Then have everyone go into the surrounding landscape to gather decorative material to weave into the braids. If you don't have enough material in the landscape or don't have access to a landscape, purchase inexpensive flowers from a local market. Everyone can wear their headbands during the Beltane celebration.

At the end of the festivities, if you have the option, take your headbands to a nearby stream, river, pond, or lake. Cast them on the water to honor the deities and the return of summer.

Yew

Latin name: Taxus

Range: Europe, Southeast Asia, North America

Parts Used: Foliage, wood

Magickal Correspondences: Feminine, water

Uses: To contact the dead, to honor chthonic deities

Edibility: No part of this plant is edible.

Warning: All parts of this plant are toxic to varying degrees.
Some people may also experience contact dermatitis from handling the plant.

Yews are part of a very old, old coniferous genus. Evidence of *Taxus* species going back 200 million years has been found. They retain that association with longevity today, with some specimen yews in Europe and England estimated to be thousands of years old.

Description

Yews are evergreens in the conifer class. The bark is red to reddish brown and thin. It tends to peel, flaking off with age. Shrub-form yews get two to 20 feet tall. Mature yews can get 50 to 80 feet tall, but they will do so very slowly.

Fresh, rich green needle foliage on yews starts life encircling the stem. In time, the formation moves to horizontal with needles on either side of the stem. The seed cones contain one seed each, wrapped in a bright red structure called an aril. If you have never seen a seed cone on your yew shrub or tree, it may be because you need a male and female plant to make that happen. An interesting fact, according to the American Conifer Society, is that occasionally a yew plant can decide to change its sex over time.[204]

History and Lore

European history in general and British Isle history in particular contain many references to historic yews. The Fortingall yew in Perthshire, Scotland, is thought to be between 2,000 and 3,000 years old. The St. Cynog Church yew in Wales is thought by some to be up to 5,000 years old. The oldest Irish yew dates back to the late 1700s. This is according to the Woodland Trust of England.[205]

Estimating the age of these old trees can be hard and some of the above listed ages could be fanciful to say the least. Arborists usually tell a tree's age by taking a core sample and counting the rings. Old yew trees have a habit of losing their heartwood. It's not fatal but it makes establishing a proper age difficult.

---

204. "Taxus Genus (Yew)," American Conifer Society, accessed August 31, 2021, https://conifersociety.org/conifers/taxus/.
205. Kylie Harrison Mellor, "Ancient Yew Trees: The UK's Oldest Yews," Woodland Trust, https://www.woodlandtrust.org.uk/blog/2018/01/ancient-yew-trees/.

Regardless, yews around the world have been treasured. Their wood has been used to make strong, flexible bows for hunting and warfare. Yew was kind of like the plastic of its day. The wood has also been used for decorative flourishes in furniture and house building.

Like the willow, the yew has a strong association with the underworld. Church graveyards around the world have yews as significant features. In some cases, the yew was a mark of everlasting life. In others, it was to keep the dead in place and away from the living.

Hecate, a chthonic Mediterranean deity, has the yew as a sacred plant. Wreaths of yew were said to have been placed on the necks of black bulls that were sacrificed in her honor.[206] Any association with Hecate is also an association with witches.

All parts of yew are toxic to humans. However, people have used it in herbal medicine in years past. This is a very bad idea to do without proper supervision of a trained herbalist due to the impact chemicals in yews have on the heart.

Modern medicine has found certain *Taxus* species contain chemicals that have cancer-fighting properties. In 1962, scientists discovered that chemicals from the Pacific yew (*T. brevifolia*) are effective against breast, ovarian, pancreatic, and non-small-cell lung cancers.[207] The drug Taxol proved so effective that Pacific yews were in serious danger of being overharvested before science was able to develop a synthetic form of the drug.

206. Della Hooke, *Trees in Anglo-Saxon England*, Anglo-Saxon Studies 13 (Suffolk, UK: Boydell Press, 2010), 207.
207. "A Story of Discovery: Natural Compound Helps Treat Breast and Ovarian Cancers," National Cancer Institute, March 31, 2015, https://www.cancer.gov/research/progress/discovery/taxol.

Uses

So many times when we do ritual or magickal work, we are asking for something from our patron deities or our ancestors. Sometimes we need to simply honor those whom we rely on every day.

You can do this with yew trees. Yew is a plant that reaches out beyond the mundane world. It reaches out across time.

You can carefully gather a few needles from the plant to blend with some boxwood leaves and myrrh resin. Yew plant material can be toxic in large-enough doses but a few teaspoons of needles will not cause you harm. Dry the needles and boxwood leaves in the oven. Once they are fully dried, grind them together and use the powder for the following ritual.

This should be done in the waning moon. It can be done with any deity you wish to honor or for any ancestors you regularly work with. When you work with Hecate, a powerful chthonic deity, it should be done at a crossroads. This doesn't have to mean a street intersection. It can mean the crossing of paths in your landscape.

Before going to your ritual space, gather a white candle and a black candle, your herb mix, and a food and drink offering for those you wish to honor. Most deities have foods that they prefer. You should also have an idea what kind of foods your ancestors might enjoy.

Once at the ritual space, establish your circle. Settle down on the ground, if possible. If not, sit at your altar. You need to be in a comfortable position. Once the ritual begins, there will be no speaking. Light the candles and begin to burn the incense. Set the food and drink out and say a prayer to those you wish to honor. Then, wait.

Those who follow Central American traditions will recognize this type of ritual because many of those cultures regularly reach out to honor and celebrate their lost loved ones. Those who follow a Celtic or Wiccan tradition will recognize this as a dumb supper. It is often done on Samhain, but you don't have to wait until October.

While you are waiting, you can pray for your loved ones who have gone beyond or silently meditate on the positive influence your patron deities have in your life. You may feel their presence. You may not. Either way, when you can no longer focus on your intent, thank those you reached out to for their help in the past. Wish them peace in their current existence. Know that you have done your part to respect those who have always been there for you. Ground yourself and open your circle.

Bibliography

Adler, Margot. *Drawing Down the Moon: Witches, Druids, Goddess-Worshippers and Other Pagans in America*. New York: Viking Press, 1979.

Aguilar-Moreno, Manuel. *Handbook to Life in the Aztec World*. New York: Facts on File, 2006.

Altman, Nathan. *Sacred Trees*. San Francisco, CA: Sierra Club Books, 1994.

Apollonius Rhodius. *The Argonautica*. Translated by R. C. Seaton. Cambridge, MA: Harvard University Press, 1912. Project Gutenberg, 2008. https://www.gutenberg.org/files/830/830-h/830-h.htm.

Appelbaum, Robert. *Aguecheek's Beef, Belch's Hiccup, and Other Gastronomic Interjections*. Chicago: University of Chicago Press, 2006.

The Aztec Empire. New York: Solomon R. Guggenheim Museum, 2004. Published in conjunction with an exhibition of the same title, organized by the Solomon R. Guggenheim Museum in collaboration with the Consejo National para la Cultura y las Artes and the Instituto Nacional de Antropologia e Historia, presented at the Solomon R. Guggenheim Museum, October 15,

2004–February 13, 2005. https://www.guggenheim.org/wp-content/uploads/2004/08/guggenheim-pub-the-aztec-empire-2004.pdf.

Balch, Phyllis A. *Prescription for Nutritional Healing.* 5th ed. New York: Penguin, 2010.

Bautista, Gabriela, Jose Jimenez, and Berna Canales. "The Human Body in Mesoamerican Ritual: Bones, Symbols and the Underworld." In *Rituals, Past, Present and Future Perspectives*, edited by Edward Bailey, chapter 4. Hauppauge, NY: Nova Science, 2017.

Berry, Thomas. *Religions of India.* Chambersburg, PA: Anima Publications, 1992.

The Bhagavad Gita. Translated by Shri Purohit Swami. HolyBooks.com. May 21, 2010. https://holybooks.com/bhagavad-gita-three-modern-translations/.

Bodi, Daniel. "The Double Current and the Tree of Healing in Ezekiel 47:1–12 in Light of Babylonian Iconography and Texts." *Die Welt Des Orients* 45, no. 1 (2015): 22–37, http://www.jstor.org/stable/43697616.

The Book of Chilam Balam of Chumayel. Translated by Ralph L. Roys. Washington, DC: Carnegie Institution, 1933.

Brennan, Martin. *The Hidden Maya.* Santa Fe, NM: Bear and Company Publishing, 1998.

Buhl, Marie-Louise. "The Goddesses of the Egyptian Tree Cult." *Journal of Near Eastern Studies* 6, no. 2 (1947): 80–97. http://www.jstor.org/stable/542585.

Bulfinch, Thomas. *The Age of Fable.* New York: New American Library, 1962.

———. *Bulfinch's Mythology*. New York: Grosset & Dunlap, 1913. Project Gutenberg, 2018.

Caldecott, Moyra. *Myths of the Sacred Tree*. Rochester, VT: Destiny Books, 1993.

Campbell, Joseph. *Primitive Mythology*. Vol. 1 of *The Masks of God*. New York: Penguin Group, 1976.

———. *Transformations of Myth Through Time*. New York: Harper & Row, 1990.

Christenson, Allen J. "The Sacred Tree of the Ancient Maya," *Journal of Book of Mormon Studies* 6, no. 1 (1997), 1–23, https:// scholarsarchive.byu.edu/jbms/vol6/iss1/2.

Cotterell, Arthur, and Rachel Storm. *The Ultimate Encyclopedia of Mythology*. New York: Hermes House, 2002.

Cunningham, Scott. *Cunningham's Encyclopedia of Magical Herbs*. St. Paul, MN: Llewellyn Publications, 1985.

Cusack, Carole. "Pagan Saxon Resistance to Charlemagne's Mission: 'Indigenous' Religion and 'World' Religion in the Early Middle Ages." *Pomegranate* 13, no. 1 (2011): 33–51. doi:10.1558/pome.v13i1.33.

———. *The Sacred Tree: Ancient and Medieval Manifestations*. Newcastle upon Tyne, UK: Cambridge Scholars Publishing, 2011.

Dalley, Stephanie, ed. and trans. *Myths from Mesopotamia: Creation, the Flood, Gilgamesh, and Others*. New York: Oxford University Press, 1989.

Davidson, H. R. Ellis. *The Road to Hel: A Study of the Conception of the Dead in Old Norse Literature*. London: Cambridge Press, 1968.

Dean, Sidney E. "Felling the Irminsul: Charlemagne's Saxon Wars." *Medieval Warfare* 5, no. 2 (2015): 15–20. https://www.jstor.org/stable/48578430.

Eliade, Mircea. *The Sacred and the Profane*. Translated by Willard R. Trask. New York: Harcourt, 1987.

Ellacombe, Henry N. *The Plant-Lore & Garden-Craft of Shakespeare*. London: Edward Arnold, 1896. Reprint, Mineola, NY: Dover Publications, 2017.

"Enki and the World Order: Translation." The Electronic Text Corpus of Sumerian Literature. University of Oxford Faculty of Oriental Studies. Last modified 2001. https://etcsl.orinst.ox.ac.uk/section1/tr113.htm.

Evelyn-White, Hugh G., trans. *Hesiod, Homeric Hymns, Epic Cycle, Homerica*. Loeb Classical Library Volume 57. London: William Heinemann, 1914.

Fallon, Nicole. "The Cross as Tree: The Wood-of-the-Cross Legends in Middle English and Latin Texts in Medieval England." Department of the Centre for Medieval Studies. PhD diss., University of Toronto, Canada, 2009.

Folkard, Richard. *Plant Lore, Legends, and Lyrics*. London: R. Folkard and Sons, 1884.

Forsyth, Mark. *A Short History of Drunkenness: How, Why, Where, and When Humankind Has Gotten Merry from the Stone Age to the Present*. New York: Three Rivers Press, 2017.

Fox, Selena. "Wiccan Shamanism." In *Circle Network News*. Mt. Horeb, WI: Circle Sanctuary, 1984. Internet Sacred Text Archive, 1999. https://www.sacred-texts.com/bos/bos046.htm.

Frazer, James. *The Golden Bough: A Study in Magic and Religion*. New York: Macmillan, 1922. Electronic reproduction, Bartleby.com, 2000. www.bartleby.com/196/.

Freidel, David, Linda Schele, and Joy Parker. *Maya Cosmos: Three Thousand Years on the Shaman's Path*. New York: William Morrow and Company, 1993.

Fried, Ellen. "Old Ironsides: Warrior and Survivor." *Prologue* 37, no. 1 (Spring 2005), n.p. https://www.archives.gov/publications/prologue/2005/spring/ironsides.html.

Geisel, Theodore Seuss. *The Lorax*. New York: Random House, 1971.

Giovino, Mariana. *The Assyrian Sacred Tree: A History of Interpretations*. Fribourg, Switzerland: Academic Press Fribourg, 2007.

Goshchytska, Tetyana. "The Tree Symbol in World Mythologies and the Mythology of the World Tree." *The Ethnology Notebooks* 3, 147 (2019), 622–40. https://nz.lviv.ua/en/2019-en-3-10/.

Gregory, Timothy. "Julian and the Last Oracle at Delphi." *Journal of Greek, Roman, and Byzantine Studies* 24, no. 4 (1983): 356. https://grbs.library.duke.edu/article/view/5801/5255.

Grieve, Maud. *A Modern Herbal*. 2 vols. New York: Dover Publications, 1971.

Hamilton, Edith. *Mythology: Timeless Tales of Gods and Heroes*. New York: New American Library, 1969. Reprint, New York: Little, Brown & Company, 1969.

Hávamál: The Words of Odin the High One from the Elder or Poetic Edda. Translated by Olive Bray. Edited by D. L. Ashliman. University of Pittsburgh. Last modified March 28, 2003. https://www.pitt.edu/~dash/havamal.html#runes.

Helgason, T., T. J. Daniell, R. Husband, A. H. Fitter, and J. P. W. Young. "Ploughing up the Wood-Wide Web?" *Nature* 394 (July 30, 1998): 431. https://www.nature.com/articles/28764.pdf.

Hesse, Hermann. *Wandering: Notes and Sketches.* Translated by James Wright. London: Pan Books, 1972.

The Holy Bible. Holman Pronouncing Edition. Philadelphia, PA: A. J. Holman Company, 1914.

Homer. *The Iliad of Homer.* Translated by Alexander Pope. London, 1899. Project Gutenberg, 2002. https://www.gutenberg.org/files/6130/6130-h/6130-h.htm.

Hooke, Della. *Trees in Anglo-Saxon England.* Anglo-Saxon Studies 13. Suffolk, UK: Boydell Press, 2010.

Hull, Eleanor, ed. *The Poem Book of the Gael, Translations from Irish Gaelic Poetry into English Prose and Verse.* London: Chatto & Windus, 1913. Project Gutenberg, 2014. https://www.gutenberg.org/files/46917/46917-h/46917-h.htm.

Illyés, Gyula. "The Tree that Reached the Sky—A Hungarian Folk Tale." Translated by Caroline Bodóczky. *Hungarian Review* 4, no. 6 (2013): n.p. http://www.hungarianreview.com/article/20131201_the_tree_that_reached_the_sky_a_hungarian_folk_tale?

Ivakhiv, Adrian. "The Revival of Ukrainian Native Faith." In *Modern Paganism in World Cultures: Comparative Perspectives,* edited by

Michael Strmiska, 209–40. Santa Barbara, CA: ABC-CLIO, 2005.

Jacobsen, Thorkild. "The Eridu Genesis." *Journal of Biblical Literature* 100, no. 4 (1981): 513–29. doi:10.2307/3266116.

James, E. O. *The Tree of Life: An Archaeological Study.* Leiden, Netherlands: Brill, 1966.

James, Jean M. "An Iconographic Study of Xiwangmu during the Han Dynasty." *Artibus Asiae* 55, no. 1/2 (1995): 17–41. https://www.jstor.org/stable/3249761.

Jung, Carl. *Aion: Researches into the Phenomenology of the Self.* Vol. 9, part 2, of *Collected Works of C. G. Jung.* Translated by R. F. C. Hull. Princeton, NJ: Princeton University Press, 1959.

———. *Nietzsche's "Zarathustra": Notes of the Seminar Given in 1934–1939.* 2 vols. Edited by James L. Jarrett. Princeton, NJ: Princeton University Press, 1988.

Karras, Ruth Mazo. "Pagan Survivals and Syncretism in the Conversion of Saxon." *The Catholic Historical Review* 72, no. 4 (1986): 553–72.

Kerven, Rosalind. *Viking Myths and Sagas.* New York: Chartwell Books, 2017.

Khalifa, Rashad, trans. *Quran: The Final Testament.* Tucson, AZ: United Submitters International, 1990.

Knowlton, Timothy, and Gabrielle Vail. "Hybrid Cosmologies in Mesoamerica: A Reevaluation of the Uax Cheel Cab, a Maya World Tree." *Ethnohistory* 57, no. 4 (Fall 2010): 709–39. doi:10.1215/00141801-2010-042.

Kramer, Samuel. *Gilgamesh and the Ḥuluppu-Tree: A Reconstructed Sumerian Text.* Chicago: University of Chicago Press, 1938.

Kure, Henning. "Hanging on the World Tree: Man and Cosmos in Old Norse Mythic Poetry." In *Old Norse Religion in Long-Term Perspectives: Origins, Changes, and Interactions,* edited by Anders Andrén, Kristina Jennbert, and Catharina Raudvere, 68–71. Lund, Sweden: Nordic Academic Press, 2006.

Langdon, S. "The Legend of the Kiskanu." *Journal of the Royal Asiatic Society of Great Britain and Ireland* 4 (1928): 843–48. http://www.jstor.org/stable/25221428.

MacCulloch, J. A. *The Religion of the Ancient Celts.* Mineola, NY: Dover Publications, 2003.

Michael, Henry, ed. *Studies in Siberian Shamanism.* Vol. 4. Toronto: University of Toronto Press, 1963.

Moore, Glenn, and Cassandra Atherton. "Eternal Forests: The Veneration of Old Trees in Japan." *Arnoldia* 77, no. 4 (2020): 24–31. https://arboretum.harvard.edu/wp-content/uploads/2020/06/2020-77-4-Arnoldia.pdf.

Nicol, D. M. "The Oracle of Dodona." *Greece & Rome* 5, no. 2 (1958): 128–43. http://www.jstor.org/stable/640927.

Osborne, William. "The Tree of Life in ancient Egypt and the Book of Proverbs." *Journal of Ancient Near Eastern Religions* 14, no. 1 (2014), 114–39. doi:10.1163/15692124-12341259.

Ovid. *Metamorphoses.* Translated by A. S. Kline. Electronic reproduction, University of Virginia, 2000. https://ovid.lib.virginia.edu/trans/Metamorph10.htm#484521420.

———. *Metamorphoses*. Translated by Rolfe Humphries. Bloomington: Indiana University Press, 1955.

Parker, Arthur. "Certain Iroquois Tree Myths and Symbols." *American Anthropologist* 14, no. 4 (Fall 1912): 608–20. https://www.jstor.org/stable/659833.

Paterson, Jacqueline Memory. *Tree Wisdom: The Definitive Guidebook to the Myth, Folklore and Healing Power of Trees*. London: Thorsons Publishing, 1996.

Pausanias. *The Description of Greece*. Vol. 2. London: R. Faulder, 1794.

Philpot, J. H. *The Sacred Tree: or, The Tree in Religion and Myth*. London: Macmillan, 1897. Project Gutenberg, 2014. https://www.gutenberg.org/files/47215/47215-h/47215-h.htm.

Pimple, Kenneth D. "Ghosts, Spirits, and Scholars: The Origins of Modern Spiritualism." In *Out of the Ordinary: Folklore and the Supernatural*, edited by Walker Barbara, 75–89. Boulder: University Press of Colorado, 1995.

Plato. *Timaeus*. Translated by Benjamin Jowett. New York: Macmillan, 1949.

Poivre, Mélanie, and Pierre Duez. "Biological Activity and Toxicity of the Chinese Herb *Magnolia officinalis* Rehder & E. Wilson (Houpo) and Its Consitutents." *Journal of Zhejiang University Science B* 18, no. 3 (2017): 194–214. doi:10.1631/jzus.B1600299.

Pseudo-Callisthenes. "Alexander Romance ('Pseudo-Callisthenes')." Attalus.org. Translated by E. H. Haight (1955), A. M. Wojohojian (1969), and E. A. W. Budge (1889). Accessed May 19, 2022. http://www.attalus.org/translate/alexander3b.html.

————. *The Romance of Alexander the Great.* Translated by Albert M. Wolohojian. New York: Columbia University Press, 1969.

Reed, Susan. "In/appropriate Education in a Time of Mass Extinction: Composing a Methodological Imbroglio of Love and Grief." EdD diss., Appalachian State University, 2015.

Saeedipour, Abass. "Dramatic Myths in the Avasto-Rig Vedic Pantheon: The Dramatic Myth of Mashya and Mashyana Revisited." Payame Noor University, Tehran. Accessed April 14, 2021. https://www.academia.edu/32003021/Dramatic_Myths _in_the_Avasto_Rig_Vedic_Pantheon_The_Dramatic_Myth _of_Mashya_and_Mashyana_Revisited?email_work_card =view-paper.

Schele, Linda, and David A. Freidel. *A Forest of Kings: The Untold Story of the Ancient Maya.* New York: William Morrow and Company, 1990.

Shorto, Russell. *Descartes' Bones.* New York: Doubleday, 2008.

Siderits, Mark. "Buddha." Stanford Encyclopedia of Philosophy. Edited by Edward N. Zalta. Last modified February 14, 2019. https://plato.stanford.edu/archives/spr2019/entries/buddha.

Smith, Ryan. *The Way of Fire and Ice: The Living Tradition of Norse Paganism.* Woodbury, MN: Llewellyn Publications, 2019.

Starhawk. *The Earth Path: Grounding Your Spirit in the Rhythm of Nature.* New York: Harper San Francisco, 2005.

Straižys, Vytautas, and Libertas Klimka. "The Cosmology of the Ancient Balts." *Journal for the History of Astronomy*, archaeoastronomy supplement 28, no. 2 (1997): S57–S81, https://doi .org/10.1177/002182869702802207.

Strmiska, Michael. "The Music of the Past in Modern Baltic Paganism." *Nova Religio: The Journal of Alternative and Emergent Religions* 8, no. 3 (2005): 39–58. https://doi.org/10.1525/nr.2005.8.3.39.

Sturluson, Snorri. *Skaldskaparmal*. In *The Prose Edda*. Translated by Arthur Gilchrist Brodeur. New York: American-Scandinavian Foundation, 1916. Sacred Texts, 2001. https://www.sacred-texts.com/neu/pre/pre05.htm.

———. *The Younger Edda, Also Called Snorre's Edda of the Prose Edda*. Translated by Rasmus Anderson. Chicago: Griggs & Co., 1879.

———. *The Younger Edda, Also Called Snorre's Edda of the Prose Edda*. Translated by Rasmus B. Anderson. Chicago: Scott, Foresman & Company, 1901. Project Gutenberg, 2006. https://www.gutenberg.org/ebooks/18947.

Stewart, Amy. *The Drunken Botanist: The Plants That Create the World's Great Drinks*. Chapel Hill, NC: Algonquin Books, 2013.

Wilkinson, Alix. *The Garden in Ancient Egypt*. London: Rubicon Press, 1998.

Wilson, Epiphanius, ed. *Egyptian Literature*. New York: The Co-Operative Publication Society, 1901.

Zaczek, Iain. *Chronicle of the Celts*. New York: Sterling, 1999.

Index

Notes

To Write to the Author

If you wish to contact the author or would like more information about this book, please write to the author in care of Llewellyn Worldwide Ltd. and we will forward your request. Both the
author and publisher appreciate hearing from you and learning of
your enjoyment of this book and how it has helped you. Llewellyn
Worldwide Ltd. cannot guarantee that every letter written to the
author can be answered, but all will be forwarded. Please write to:

JD Walker
℅ Llewellyn Worldwide
2143 Wooddale Drive
Woodbury, MN 55125-2989

Please enclose a self-addressed stamped envelope for reply,
or $1.00 to cover costs. If outside the U.S.A., enclose
an international postal reply coupon.

Many of Llewellyn's authors have websites with additional information and resources. For more information, please visit our website
at http://www.llewellyn.com.